The U.S. Estate and Gift Tax
and the Non-Citizen

The U.S. Estate and Gift Tax and the Non-Citizen

SECOND EDITION

ISBN: 978-0-9882183-4-5

CONTENTS

INTRODUCTION

A large part of our practice is devoted to the service of foreign nationals and U.S. investors with foreign ties. Some of our multinational clients and their financial and legal advisors have asked that we develop a concise book explaining the impact of the U.S. estate and gift tax on non-citizens. The book covers some of the pertinent death and gift tax issues facing resident and non-resident foreign nationals. This second edition includes a more expansive explanation of several topics but remains only an introduction to a complex area of law and cannot be relied on as legal advice applicable to any specific circumstance.

OVERVIEW OF THE U.S. ESTATE AND GIFT TAX

Since 1916, the United States has imposed an "Estate Tax"[1] on the U.S. assets of foreign decedents and on all assets of U.S. citizens and residents. The tax covers transfers of wealth at death. The U.S. also imposes a "Gift Tax"[2] on gratuitous lifetime transfers. Gift Tax covers the value of gifts made during life. Non-resident non-citizens are taxed only on gifts of U.S. based assets.[3]

Since 1977, the Gift Tax and the Estate Tax have been integrated for U.S. citizens and residents. The value of both taxable gifts and taxable estate assets may be offset to the extent of the "unified credit" against both Estate and Gift Tax. Lifetime gifts of property (to the extent exceeding the $15,000 annual exemption for each donee)[4] are taxable but reduce the grantor's

---

[1] Internal Revenue Code §2001 (hereinafter "IRC").
[2] IRC §2501.
[3] IRC §2511.
[4] IRC §2503 (applicable to U.S. residents and non-resident non-citizens ("NRNCs").

3

taxable estate (at death).[5] Tax on lifetime gifts may be offset by the unified credit, but lifetime use of the credit reduces the credit available at death. The estate of a U.S. decedent is afforded the remaining "unified credit" against both Estate Tax and Gift Tax.

The unified credit "exempts" from taxation the value of property up to the "applicable exclusion amount."[6] For calendar year 2019, the exclusion amount for U.S. citizens and residents is $11,400,000 per individual.[7]

> Gift or Estate Tax is only owed by U.S. residents and citizens if the aggregate value of all lifetime gifts (exceeding $15,000 per donee per year) and all testamentary bequests (i.e., gifts at death) exceed the unified credit.

---

[5] Beginning on January 1, 1977, the tax was calculated on the combined value of an individual's "taxable estate" (generally assets which the decedent owned or controlled, less certain deductions allowed by the Internal Revenue Code), and an individual's "adjusted taxable gifts" (i.e., gifts not included in the "taxable estate").

[6] IRC §2010(c)(2).

[7] The applicable exclusion amount is indexed for inflation on an annual basis.

4

Currently, the rate of tax for both Gift Tax and Estate Tax is 40% of the value of property transferred.[8]

<u>Non-Resident Non-Citizens</u>

The Estate Tax exemption for non-resident non-citizens ("NRNCs") is only $60,000.[9] The NRNC may not apply the $60,000 credit against taxable lifetime gifts.[10] Gift Tax is, therefore, due on all lifetime gifts exceeding the $15,000 annual exemption.

Gifts to one's U.S. citizen spouse are, however, not taxable (for both U.S. and non-U.S. grantors). The exemption for lifetime gifts to non-citizen spouses is, however, limited to $149,000 annually.[11] A few U.S. tax treaties include a gift tax marital deduction for transfers to noncitizen spouses. If a treaty

---

[8] Although IRC §2001(c) provides a "rate schedule" for the imposition of the tax, the highest marginal rate is imposed beginning with estates valued over one million dollars. As the current exemption amount is in excess of eleven million dollars, the Estate Tax essentially functions as a "flat tax" at the top marginal rate.
[9] IRC §2102(b)(1).
[10] IRC §2523(a), (i).
[11] IRC §2523(i)(2).

applies, the limited annual exclusion can be avoided. See page 65 below, regarding Estate and Gift Tax Treaties.

The rate of Gift and Estate Tax on NRNCs is the same as that applied to U.S. grantors. If applicable, U.S. estate and gift tax treaties (discussed on page 68 below) diminish the Estate and Gift Tax imposed on non-citizens.

Tax Basis

The tax treatment of property inherited by an heir can be very distinct from the tax treatment of property received as a gift. The tax basis received in property (as a gift or inherited) impacts the tax owing on a later sale of the property. Recipients of (i) property inherited from a U.S. citizen or resident or (ii) U.S. situs property inherited from an NRA, receive a "stepped-up" income tax "basis" on the inherited property.

> The "step-up" adjusts the tax basis of property
> inherited to the fair market value of the property (as
> of the date of the decedent's death).[12]

If for any reason the property is valued lower than the donor's tax basis at the time of inheritance, the decedent receives a "step-down" basis in the property.

The step-up in tax basis of inherited property allows the heirs to avoid having to pay (in the event of a subsequent sale of the property) tax on any prior appreciation. In contrast, the recipient of a lifetime gift receives a tax basis equal to the lower of (i) the tax basis held by the grantor or (ii) the fair market value of the property at the time of the gift.[13] If the expected "step-up" to fair market value is substantial, it may be prudent to defer certain gifts until death.

---

[12] IRC §1014(a)(1).
[13] IRC §1015(a).

7

DETERMINING U.S. ESTATE TAX STATUS

The impact of the Estate Tax depends on whether an individual decedent is a U.S. citizen, a U.S. resident or a NRNC. Status as a citizen, resident or NRNC is significant because the Estate Tax is far more expansive as applied to citizens and residents (as opposed to NRNCs).

Definition of U.S. Citizenship

U.S. citizenship may be obtained by birth or naturalization.[14] Citizenship is granted by the 14th Amendment to the United States Constitution. "All persons born or naturalized in the United States, and subject to the jurisdiction thereof, are citizens of the United States and of the state wherein they reside."[15] For purposes of birthright citizenship, the definition of "United States" includes the fifty states, Puerto Rico, Guam, the Virgin Islands, and the Commonwealth of the Northern Mariana

---

[14] *United States v. Wong Kim Ark,* 169 U.S. 649, 702 (1898).
[15] U.S. Const. amend. XIV, §1.

9

Islands.[16] Birthright citizenship is unrelated to intent and applies even when neither parent is a U.S. citizen or resident.[17] The rule operates independently of citizenship rules of other countries[18] and extends to people born in the United States who never reside (or intended to reside) in the U.S.[19] As such, it is possible to inadvertently acquire U.S. citizenship, due purely to the timing of parental travel.

Non-Citizens: Residency and the Concept of Domicile

The Internal Revenue Code speaks of U.S. "residents" and "non-residents" regarding the Estate and Gift Tax. The Code, however, contains no definition of "resident" or "residency" applicable to the imposition of Estate or Gift Tax. Instead, Estate Tax regulations require a determination of whether an individual has established "domicile" in the U.S.[20]

---

[16] 8 USC §1101(a)(38).
[17] *U.S. v. Wong Kim Ark*, 169 U.S. 649 (1898).
[18] *Perkins v. Elg*, 307 U.S. 325, 329 (1939).
[19] An individual can renounce their citizenship, most commonly by making a renunciation before a U.S. diplomat abroad. 8 USC §1481(a)(5).
[20] Treas. Reg. §20.0-1(b)(1).

> The regulations state that "a person acquires domicile in a place by living there, for even a brief period of time, with no definite present intention of later removing therefrom."[21]

To prove that an individual is domiciled in the U.S. (i.e., a "resident" for Estate and Gift Tax purposes), two elements must be proven. The first is whether a person has or had a physical presence in the U.S. The second element hinges on the individual's intent to remain in the United States. As this second element requires a case-by-case examination of intent, [22] categorization can be unpredictable.[23]

---

[21] *Id.*

[22] *Carrasco- Favela v. INS,* 563 F.2d 1220 (5th Cir. 1977). *See also, Mas v. Perry,* 5 Cir., 1974, 489 F.2d 1396, *cert. denied,* 419 U.S. 842, 95 S. Ct. 74, 42 L. Ed. 2d 70; *Garner v. Pearson,* M.D.Fla., 1973, 374 F. Supp. 580, 589-90.

[23] *Bowring v. Bowers,* 24 F.2d 918 (Court held that despite evidence indicating the taxpayer's desire and intention to return to England he had established a residence "of no transient character and... so substantial as to be of a permanent nature" and thus determined the taxpayer to be a resident alien).

The intent to establish domicile is a state of mind, proven by facts and circumstances. Factors include: (i) the time spent in the U.S. and abroad; (ii) the financial investment and location of the decedent's home; (iii) the place of business operations; (iv) U.S. visa and immigration status; (v) the reason for spending time in the U.S. (i.e., healthcare, tourism or asylum); (vi) the residence of friends and family; (vii) the place of religious and social affiliations; (viii) the residence reflected in legal documents; (ix) place of voter registration and driver's license and (x) residence status disclosed on tax filings.[24]

---

[24] See *Estate of Valentine v. Commissioner*, 21 B.T.A. 197 (1930), *acq.* X-1 C.B. 4., 67; *Jellinek v. Commissioner*, 36 T.C. 826 (1961), *acq.* 1964-1 C.B. 4.; *Estate of Bloch-Sulzberger*, 6 T.C.M. 1201, 1203 (1974); *Estate of Nienhuys*, 17 T. C. 1149, 159 (1952); *Estate of Paquette*, T.C. Memo. 1983-571.

The U.S. income tax rules for determining residency are distinct from the Estate Tax rules.[25] An individual may therefore be a resident for income tax purposes but not for Estate Tax purposes and vice versa.

Once domicile is established (for Estate Tax purposes), it is presumed to continue until shown to have changed.[26] If an individual previously established U.S. domicile, the burden will be on the party asserting non-U.S. domicile to prove a change in status.[27] Several court cases address the issue.

In *Estate of Khan v. C.I.R.*[28] the decedent, a citizen of Pakistan, was held to be a U.S. resident at the time of his death. The decedent had substantial ownership interests in a ranching business and a residential real estate enterprise in California (both

---

[25] IRC §7701(b).
[26] *Estate of Nienhuys v. Comr.*, 17 T.C. 1149 (1952).
[27] *Id.*
[28] *Estate of Khan v. C.I.R.*, 75 TCM 1597 (1998).

of which were initially purchased by the decedent's father). The decedent applied for a U.S. social security number and green card to preserve subsidies given by the U.S. Department of Agriculture to the decedent's farming operation. Although the decedent spent the vast majority of his life in Pakistan, died without knowing English, and spent fourteen of his last eighteen years exclusively in Pakistan (all of which suggest no intention to permanently reside in the U.S.), the U.S. Tax Court treated him as a resident for Estate Tax purposes.

The court placed substantial weight on the fact that (i) the vast majority of the decedent's business assets were located in the U.S., (ii) the decedent had obtained a green card and social security number, and (iii) the decedent had applied for a U.S. re-entry permit prior to his last trip to Pakistan (although he never returned to the U.S.). The Tax Court noted that the decedent would have returned to the U.S. but for a debilitating medical condition. Curiously, the court also seemed to give weight to the fact that the taxpayer's family had a history of immigrating to the

United States. This family history factor may be a cause for concern from a planning perspective because the intentions of other individuals were apparently imputed to the taxpayer.[29]

Conversely, in the case of *Estate of Paquette v. Comr.*[30], a Canadian citizen split his time between Quebec, Canada and Florida. Although, at the time of his death, the taxpayer owned no physical residence in Canada, the Tax Court determined that he was a non-resident for U.S. Estate Tax purposes. The Court based its determination on the facts that the decedent (i) chose to reside in Florida instead of Canada for health reasons (the cold weather adversely impacted his medical condition), (ii) maintained investment accounts in Canada, (iii) voted in Canada, (iv) maintained a Canadian driver's license, (v) registered his vehicle in Canada and (vi) executed his will in Canada. This case stands for the proposition that the location of a physical residence

---

[29] Although the taxpayer in this case actually sought to be treated as a resident, this case may be viewed as a "trap" for those intending to avoid residency.

[30] *Estate of Paquette v. Comr.*, 46 TCM 1400 (1983).

does not by itself create a presumption of domicile; rather, "it is merely one of several factors which must be examined to ascertain [a] decedent's intent."[31]

Likewise, in the case of *Forni v. Comr.*,[32] the taxpayer was a citizen and resident of Italy. The taxpayer's wife died with property located in the U.S. As a result of a Presidential Order issued during World War II, the trust company which held the wife's assets was prohibited from releasing the property to the taxpayer.[33]

The taxpayer had moved to the U.S. claiming residency, but correspondence with his U.S. attorneys revealed he had no intention of staying in the U.S. longer than necessary to free the assets (and return to his native Italy). The Tax Court held that the decedent lacked the requisite intent to change his domicile and remained a non-resident for U.S. Estate Tax purposes.

---

[31] *Id.*
[32] *Forni v. Comr.*, 22 T.C. 975 (1954).
[33] *Id.* at 977.

These cases demonstrate the fact-intensive nature of determining a person's domicile. Domicile should be clearly established prior to undertaking estate planning.

ESTATE AND GIFT TAX IMPOSED ON U.S. CITIZENS AND RESIDENT NON-CITIZENS

"Worldwide Assets"

The U.S. Estate Tax is imposed on the "Gross Estate" of U.S. Citizens and U.S. residents.[34]

> The Gross Estate of a U.S. person includes "the value at the time of his death of all property, real or personal, tangible or intangible, wherever situated".[35]

This phrase, "wherever situated," imposes the Estate and Gift Tax on "worldwide assets." The Estate Tax and the Gift Tax attach to all assets regardless of the location of the U.S. citizen or resident (or his property) at the time of gift or death. Citizens and non-citizen residents are afforded a unified credit against Estate and Gift Tax, which currently "shields" $11,490,000 in assets. No Gift Tax or Estate Tax is actually payable by U.S. citizens and

---

[34] IRC §2001.
[35] IRC §2031(a).

19

residents until the value of lifetime gifts and bequests exceed the unified credit.

U.S. citizens and residents generally receive a credit for estate tax paid to a foreign country on property subject to the Estate Tax.[36] Note that the credit may be altered by any applicable estate tax treaty. See page 39 below.

Completion of Gifts

To complete a gift for Estate and Gift Tax purposes, the transferor must retain no right to change the disposition of the property transferred.[37] If, for example, the transferor retains the right to name new beneficiaries of a donee trust or change the proportionate benefit of trust beneficiaries, such retained powers may cause the gift to be treated as "incomplete."

Gifts generally remain incomplete if the transferor retains the power to alter beneficial interests in the property (as opposed to retaining rights over the manner or time of enjoyment of the

------

[36] IRC §20014.
[37] Treas. Reg. §25.2511-2(b).

property). By reserving the right to alter beneficial interests, the transferor has not truly parted with dominion and control of the transferred property. The Gift Tax does not apply to such incomplete gifts.[38] Incomplete gifts remain in the taxable estate of the donor.

Technically, the Code makes gifts to trusts "incomplete" when the transferor reserves rights to: (1) change beneficial title to trust property (both income and principal), (2) name new trust beneficiaries, or (3) change the interests of beneficiaries as between themselves (except when the change in interest is limited by a fixed or ascertainable standard).

Gifts in trust limiting trustee discretion to a fixed or ascertainable standard (for distributions) are considered complete. Trusts so limiting trustee discretion are deemed to eliminate grantor rights to alter beneficial interests in trust assets. This is true even if the grantor is the trustee. An example of a fixed and ascertainable standard for distribution is the condition that

---

[38] Treas. Reg. §25.2511-2(c).

distributions must be made for the health, support, education, or maintenance of the permissible beneficiaries. Gifts to trust requiring support distributions are considered "completed" gifts because the transferor has relinquished sufficient dominion and control over the transferred asset. The exception to trustee discretion for support distributions allows the transferor to complete a transfer yet serve as a fiduciary (i.e. trustee) over the transferred assets.

The subsequent relinquishment or termination of a retained power (which prevented completion of the gift) during the donor's lifetime will complete the gift and trigger Gift Tax.[39] In the event a trust (holding incomplete gifts) makes unfettered distributions of income or principal (during the transferor's lifetime), such trust distributions are considered completed taxable gifts by the grantor to the receiving beneficiaries.[40]

---

[39] Treas. Reg. §25.2511-2(f).
[40] Treas. Reg. §25.2511-2(b).

Estate and Gift Tax Consequences of Completed Gifts

If a U.S. person creates a trust benefitting someone else, parts with dominion and control over transferred property (leaving him with no power to change its disposition), the Gift Tax will apply to such transfer. The Settlor may use his unified credit to offset the Gift Tax otherwise due. See page 3. In 2019, the unified credit provides a $11,490,000 Gift Tax exemption. To the extent that the value of assets transferred to the irrevocable trust (foreign or domestic) exceeds $11,490,000, a 40% tax (Gift Tax or GST, or both, as the case may be) is imposed on the Settlor.

Transfers Between U.S. Citizen Spouses

U.S. citizens may delay the imposition of either the Gift Tax or the Estate Tax on transfers between citizen spouses.

> If both spouses are citizens of the United States, either spouse may transfer assets to the other spouse and receive a tax deduction for the entire value of the property transferred.[41]

Such transfers may be accomplished during life or at death and either by outright gift or through gifts in trust (for the benefit of the other spouse).

The first spouse to die may leave his or her entire estate to the surviving U.S. citizen spouse without triggering the Estate Tax (payable on the death of the second spouse).[42] Thus, any Estate Tax owed by the first spouse to die may be delayed (by devising the deceased's estate to the surviving spouse). This concept is known as the "unlimited" marital deduction.

---

[41] IRC §2523(a) and (i); §2056(a).
[42] IRC §2056. Under this code section, a deduction is allowed for "*any interest in property* (emphasis added) which passes or has passed from the decedent to his surviving spouse". (emphasis added).

A U.S. citizen or resident may also "port" his or her individual exclusion amount (currently $11,400,000[43]) to the surviving spouse. Any exclusion amount not used by the first spouse to die (by lifetime and testamentary non-spousal gifts) may be transferred (or "ported") to the qualifying surviving spouse.[44] The total amount of property excluded from the Estate Tax ($11,400,000 times two, or $22,800,000) may therefore be "pooled" by U.S. spouses (and applied against the taxable estate of the second spouse to die).

Certain limitations are, however, imposed on the marital deduction for property transferred to a non-U.S. citizen spouse (even if the recipient spouse is a U.S. resident). The restrictions are discussed in the following sections.

---

[43] IRC §2010(c)(3)(A), (B).
[44] IRC §2010(c)(4).

TESTAMENTARY TRANSFERS TO NON-CITIZEN SPOUSES

Marital Deduction for Bequests

The unlimited marital deduction for estate assets of a U.S. citizen or resident (left to a surviving spouse) is restricted for surviving non-citizen spouses. A surviving non-citizen spouse may not generally receive a bequest (from a citizen or resident deceased spouse) tax-free.[45] The restriction is intended to limit the risk of the surviving non-citizen spouse (even if a U.S. resident) leaving the U.S. with the decedent's taxable estate. A shift in domicile by the surviving (non-citizen) spouse could allow for avoidance of Estate Tax, as the survivor (with the estate assets) could permanently leave the U.S. and elude Estate Tax on "worldwide" assets. Titling (during marriage) marital assets (especially assets not located in the U.S.) in the name of the non-citizen spouse should be considered if the intention is for the

---

[45] IRC §2056(d)(1).

survivor to leave the U.S. A NRNC surviving spouse is subject to Estate Tax only on U.S. situs assets.

Qualified Domestic Trusts

Any U.S. citizen or resident may defer Estate Tax on testamentary transfers to a non-citizen spouse through a special trust. The grantor spouse must leave his or her estate to a "qualified domestic trust" ("QDOT"),[46] as a condition to receiving the marital deduction. The fiduciary of the estate must make the QDOT election on the deceased spouse's Estate Tax return.

> In the absence of an Estate Tax treaty, only through the QDOT may Estate Tax (on assets held by a U.S. citizen or resident spouse) be deferred until the death of a surviving non-citizen spouse.

Transfers to QDOTs thus qualify for the marital deduction. Distributions from a QDOT of trust principal are

---

[46] IRC §2056(d)(2)(A); §2056A.

subject to the Estate Tax. To qualify for the marital deduction, the deceased's property must pass either (i) directly to a QDOT before filing the deceased's estate tax return,[47] or (ii) from the NRNC recipient spouse (to the QDOT) within nine months of the decedent's death.

Restrictions limit who may act as a QDOT trustee. Trustee distributions are also restricted, to insure payment of U.S. income tax [48] (with certain exclusions for QDOTs with minimal assets and for QDOTs holding the personal residence of the non-citizen spouse).

If the surviving non-citizen spouse becomes a U.S. citizen before the deceased's Estate Tax return is filed, direct bequests to the survivor will qualify for the marital deduction. If the surviving spouse later becomes a U.S. citizen, all QDOT assets may then be distributed directly to the survivor (free of tax, through the marital deduction).

---

[47] §2056(d).
[48] Reg. §20.2056A-2.

29

To qualify for the marital deduction, the QDOT must (i) be executed under U.S. law,[49] (ii) have at least one trustee that is a U.S. citizen or U.S. corporation, and (iii) not allow for distributions unless the trustee has the right to withhold tax on transfers from the trust to the surviving (non-citizen) spouse.[50] The executor of the first spouse to die must elect to treat the trust as a QDOT and pass property directly to the QDOT.[51] Certain other mandatory trustee powers must be included to allow for certain restrictions to secure U.S. tax compliance.

Any distributions of principal from the QDOT to the surviving noncitizen spouse are subject to the Estate Tax at the time of distribution. Any principal remaining at the death of the non-citizen spouse will also be subject to Estate Tax (as part of the estate of the first spouse to die). Distributions of income are not subject to the Estate Tax.[52]

---

[49] Treas. Reg. §20-2056A-2(a).
[50] IRC §2056(a)(1)B).
[51] IRC §2056(d)(2)(B); Treas. Reg. §20.2056A-2(b)(2).
[52] IRC §2056A(b)(3)(A).

Treasury regulations permit a modified "portability" election to be made (to allow a surviving non-citizen spouse to utilize the deceased's unused Estate Tax exemption).[53] Estates of NRNC spouses may not, however, elect portability.[54]

The modified portability credit (applied through the QDOT) delays imposition of Estate Tax until the death of the second (non-citizen) spouse. Upon the death of the non-citizen spouse, the first spouse's unused Estate Tax exemption is applied. The determination of the amount of exemption (left by the first spouse to die) involves a series of valuation procedures. The formula is influenced by the appreciation or depreciation of assets in the QDOT.

Rules of administration exempt the QDOT from "foreign trust" status (and the associated onerous reporting requirements).[55]

---

[53] Treas. Reg. §20.2010-2(a)(5).
[54] Treas. Reg. §20.2010-2(c)(4).
[55] IRC §7701(a)(30), IRC §7701(a)(31); Treas. Reg. §301.7701-7(d)(4) ex. 2-4.

LIFETIME GIFTS TO CITIZEN
AND NON-CITIZEN SPOUSES

Only citizens enjoy an unlimited deduction (i.e., no tax imposed) for lifetime spousal gifts.[56] Similar to the restriction on tax-free testamentary gifts to non-citizen spouses, tax-free lifetime gifts are also limited.

> If the spouse receiving a lifetime gift is not a U.S. citizen, the gifting spouse may only deduct $149,000 in tax-free spousal gifts during any calendar year.[57]

The limitation on lifetime gifts applies even if both spouses are domiciled in the U.S. at the time of the gift. The domicile of the donor and donee is irrelevant. Annual lifetime gifts to non-citizen spouses are thus taxed on value exceeding $149,000 (adjusted annually for inflation). Interestingly, the

---

[56] IRC §2523(i).
[57] IRC §2523(i)(2). The deduction was initially set at $100,000 in 1989, indexed for inflation.

limitation on gifts to non-citizen spouses does not limit tax-free gifts by a non-citizen spouse to a U.S. citizen spouse. A NRNC considering U.S. residency should generally make any intended large spousal gifts of foreign property and U.S. intangible property (free of Estate and Gift Tax) before moving to the U.S. Once domiciled in the U.S., the grantor is subject to the Gift Tax on all assets held worldwide and the $149,000 limited deduction on spousal gifts (to a non-citizen spouse).

To avoid Gift Tax on spousal gifts to a foreign spouse, a U.S. spouse may: (i) make gifts through shared title, as tenants by the entireties (if available) or joint tenancy with rights of survivorship; (ii) apply (to the extent available) his or her remaining Estate and Gift Tax exclusion (against the value of gifts exceeding the limitation on gifts to a non-citizen spouse); or (iii) defer the spousal gift until death. Unfortunately, joint titling will only defer transfer tax until the death of the donor spouse, when Estate Tax is due on all jointly titled U.S. situs assets (unless contributed to a QDOT).[58] Deferral of the gift until death will potentially avoid Estate Tax entirely through either (i) testamentary transfers to a QDOT trust (explained on page 28 above) or (ii) applying the grantor's Estate Tax Credit (to the extent sufficient to cover the value of the gift).[59]

---

[58] IRC §2040(a); *see also*, Treas. Reg. §20.2056A-8.
[59] *Id.*

ESTATE TAX IMPOSED ON
NON-RESIDENT NON-CITIZENS

Property "Situated in the United States"

The Estate Tax imposed on NRNCs [60] is limited to property owned "which at the time of the NRNC's death is situated in the United States."[61] The NRNC receives a tax credit (against the Estate Tax) for any tax paid to a foreign jurisdiction arising on the death and imposed on the value of the decedent's assets.[62] The U.S. taxable estate of a NRNC also includes U.S.

---

[60] IRC §2101.
[61] IRC §2103.
[62] Rev. Rul. 82-82, 1982-1 C.B. 127; *see also* IRC §2014.

assets held in a foreign or U.S. trust generally controlled by or accessible to the NRNC.[63]

> To avoid the Estate Tax, the NRNC should avoid owning or controlling assets "situated" in the United States.

To determine where an asset is "situated," one must first look to the U.S. Treasury Regulations which deem certain assets

---

[63] *See* Treas. Reg §20.2104-1(a). Some countries do not impose estate or inheritance taxes while other countries have Estate Taxes which are imposed on relatively small wealth transfers. For example, the maximum rate imposed by the Brazilian version of an Estate Tax (the Brazilian "Imposto sobre Transmissã Causea Mortis e Doação," or ITCMD) is 8%; however, the threshold for the imposition of the tax is substantially lower than in the United States. In Sao Paulo, the tax is imposed on all transfers exceeding 40,000 Brazilian reals (approximately $14,000 U.S. Dollars) and in Mineas Gerais, on all transfers exceeding 20,000 Brazilian Reals.

U.S. "situs" property.[65] Assets deemed located in the U.S. include U.S. real estate, stock in U.S. corporations and certain tangible personal property.[66] Determining the "situs" of other assets is a more factual inquiry.[67] Factors include the owner's rights to the asset and the connections between the asset and a given country.

Rate of Estate Tax and Credit

The rate of Estate Tax imposed on NRNCs is identical to that imposed on U.S. citizens and U.S. residents.[68] The Estate Tax credit for NRNCs is significantly lower than the credit allowed U.S. citizens and residents.[69]

---

[65] *Id.*

[66] IRC §2014; Treas. Reg. §§20.2104-1, 20.2105-1. (with respect to property not deemed located within the U.S.).

[67] *Id.*

[68] IRC §2101(b)(1).

[69] IRC §2102(b)(1). Unlike the applicable exclusion amount afforded to U.S. citizens and residents, the amount for NRNCs is not indexed for inflation.

> NRNCs are allowed only a $13,000 credit against
> the Estate Tax[70] (which shields $60,000 of U.S.
> situs property).[71] The credit may not be applied
> against taxable gifts.

Marital bequests are not taxable but (as discussed at page 28 above) non-citizen spouses must receive testamentary gifts through a QDOT trust. The estate of a NRNC may not elect portability of any unused Estate Tax credit to the surviving spouse.[72]

---

[70] *Id.*
[71] IRC §2001(c).
[72] Treas. Reg. §20.2010-2(a)(5).

GIFT TAX IMPOSED ON
NON-RESIDENT NON-CITIZENS

NRNCs are subject to U.S. Gift Tax on U.S. assets. Intangible assets are, however, excluded.[73]

> A non-resident non-citizen may make unlimited gifts of U.S. stocks and bonds free of Gift Tax.

Although neither Congress nor the IRS has defined "intangible property," case law allows for certain generalizations. Assets whose value is derived from contract law or a cause of action similar to contract law are considered intangible property.[74] Such assets include annuities, shares of

---

[73] IRC §2501(a)(2).
[74] *Pilgrim's Price Corp. v. C.I.R.*, 141 TC 553 (2013); *Burnett v. Wells*, 289 U.S. 670 (1933).

stock, membership interests and other entity ownership rights.[75] Life insurance policies[76] qualify as intangible property.[77]

Interestingly, if U.S. securities (or other intangible U.S. assets) are not given away during life, they become subject to Estate Tax upon the NRNC owner's death. To minimize Estate Tax (ultimately payable on death), NRNCs should make lifetime transfers of U.S. intangible property. Note that gifts of currency within the U.S. are taxed as gifts of tangible property.[78] Such taxable gifts include cash gifts; deposits on account at a U.S. bank transferred to another U.S. bank (by check or wire transfer); and

---

[75] See PLR 9347014, where the IRS ruled that a gift by a Canadian resident-citizen of stock owned in a Canadian corporation was not subject to the Gift Tax.
[76] *Id.*
[77] *Citizens Bank of Maryland v. Strumpf,* 516 U.S. 16 (1995); *IT&S of Iowa, Inc. v. C.I.R.,* 97 T.C. 496 (1991); PLR 8210055, PLR 773706. Note the distinction between bank deposits (intangible) with physical dollar bills which are held in a safe deposit box (tangible).
[78] See GCM 36860 (Nov. 24, 1976).

deposits with a domestic branch of a foreign bank, if such branch is engaged in the commercial banking business.[79]

NRNC gifts of tangible U.S. property are taxed to the extent of value exceeding $15,000 (per donee per year).[80] Smaller gifts fall within the annual Gift Tax exclusion. Unlike gifts made by U.S. residents or citizens, Gift Tax incurred by NRNCs may not be offset against the Estate Tax credit.[81]

There are also significant restrictions on tax-free lifetime gifts to non-citizen spouses. The most significant is the absence of the "unlimited" lifetime marital deduction (discussed at page 27 above).

Generation-Skipping Transfer (GST) Tax [82] is also relevant to transfers made by a NRNC. A NRNC transferor is subject to GST tax for any transfer of assets subject to Estate or

---

[79] IRC §2104(c). *See also*, Treas. Reg. §20.2105-1 (tangible property located outside the U.S. is considered situated outside of the U.S. and not subject to tax).
[80] IRC §2503(b)(1).
[81] IRC §2505.
[82] IRC §2601.

Gift Tax which skips the next generation.[83] A NRNC transferor is allowed a GST exemption of $1,000,000.[84]

---

[83] *Id.*; *see also* Treas. Reg §26.2663-2(b)(1).
[84] Treas. Reg. §26.2663-2(a).

UNIQUE ASSET CONSIDERATIONS FOR
NON-RESIDENT NON-CITIZENS

Transfers of Intangible Property

As noted above, U.S. Gift Tax does not apply to lifetime transfers of "intangible property" by NRNCs.[85] The rule allows for avoidance of the Estate Tax through lifetime gifts of U.S. intangible property (otherwise subject to Estate Tax upon the death of the NRNC).[86] NRNCs may therefore reduce their taxable estate by making lifetime transfers of U.S. intangibles.

Note that certain U.S. intangible assets are excluded from Estate Tax (even if owned by the NRNC at death). These

---

[85] IRC §2501(a)(2).
[86] Treas. Reg. §20.2105-1(e), Treas. Reg. §20.2104-1(a)(4) includes in the estate of a NRNC "intangible personal property the written evidence of which is not treated as being the property itself, if it is not issued by or enforceable against a resident of the United States or a domestic corporation or governmental unit." Thus, if the intangible personal property is enforceable against or issued by a U.S. resident, domestic corporation, or governmental unit, it will be treated as located within the U.S. and brought within the NRNC's gross estate under the "situs" rule.

exclusions are integral to U.S. Estate Tax planning for NRNCs and are discussed below.

Bank Deposits

Cash deposits by NRNCs in U.S. banks are not subject to Estate Tax, provided that the deposits are "not effectively connected with the conduct of a trade or business in the United States." [87] Deposits connected with a U.S. trade or business (owned by a NRNC) are excluded from Estate Tax if held in foreign or offshore branches of domestic banks. [88] Deposits owned by a NRNC at a U.S. branch of a foreign bank are, however, subject to Estate Tax, "whether or not the decedent was engaged in business in the United States at the time of his death."[89]

---

[87] IRC §2105(b)(1), by cross reference, excludes amounts not effectively connected with the conduct of a trade or business within the United States, provided such amounts are deposited with entities which are (A) engaged in the banking business, (B) are chartered as savings and loans institutions or similar associations or (C) are held by an insurance company with an agreement to pay interest on those deposits. *See also*, IRC §871(i).

[88] IRC §2105(b)(2).

[89] Treas. Reg. §20.2104-1(a)(8).

To qualify as a bank "deposit," the account must be maintained "on behalf of, or 'for' the decedent,"[90] meaning that the decedent must have had a direct and enforceable claim on the specific account.[91]

The concept of having a direct and enforceable claim is addressed in the case of *Estate of Ogarrio v. C.I.R.*[92] The decedent, a non-resident Mexican citizen, was owed money by a brokerage house (from a stock sale). The brokerage house put the sale proceeds into a general account, from which the broker could pay a variety of obligations (not solely the broker's obligation to disburse proceeds to the decedent). The decedent's estate argued that the "cash account" constituted an excluded "deposit" (not subject to Estate Tax).

The Tax Court ruled that the brokerage house was not a bank, concluding that the "cash account" was not a deposit account but rather a general liability of the brokerage to the

---

[90] *Estate of Ogarrio v. C.I.R.*, 40 T.C. 242, 248 (1963).
[91] *Id.*
[92] *Id.*

decedent.[93] The decedent had only a general claim against the debtor for non-payment (rather than an enforceable claim against a specific account).[94]

> To establish an exempt bank account, the decedent must own or control the account (i.e., have the right to unfettered demand of funds held in the account).

This position is supported by the case of *Estate of Gade v. C.I.R.* [95] which expanded the meaning of "deposit" from conventional savings and checking accounts to custodial accounts. The decedent in *Gade* opened an account with a trust company and executed an agreement, which made the trust company both the agent and custodian of the account. The court concluded that, although the trust company managed the funds, the decedent's

---

[93] *Id.* at 246.
[94] *Id.* at 247.
[95] *Gade v. Commissioner,* 10 T.C. 585 (1948).

directives (in the agency agreement) qualified the account as a "deposit."

Note that a "deposit" is distinct from U.S. paper currency on hand in a physical location. Money is generally treated as a tangible asset which (if transferred by a NRNC in the U.S.) is subject to Gift Tax (on transfer) and Estate Tax (on death).[96] Gifts of paper currency by a NRNC should therefore be made outside the U.S.

U.S. Bonds

U.S. government and corporate bonds considered so-called "portfolio debt" are exempt from Estate Tax.[97] Although the definition of portfolio debt is somewhat ambiguous, bonds issued by the U.S. government and publicly traded U.S. entities are generally excluded from the taxable estate of a NRNC

---

[96] Rev. Rul. 55-143 (holding that the cash in the safe-deposit box on the date of decedent's death were not "moneys deposited" with a person carrying on the banking business within the meaning of section 863(b) of the IRC of 1939, and were thus includible in the decedent's gross estate situated in the U.S.); *See* Rev. Rul. 55-143.
[97] IRC §2105(b)(3).

owner/lender. Debt owed by NRNCs is considered a non-U.S. situs asset.

Life Insurance

Life insurance proceeds received by the estate of a NRNC (insured by such policy) are not subject to Estate Tax.[98] The Internal Revenue Code explicitly states that life insurance proceeds insuring the life of a NRNC "shall not be deemed property within the United States."[99] Proceeds are therefore not included in the estate of the NRNC owner/insured. This makes life insurance a very attractive asset.

The life insurance exclusion does not apply to the cash surrender value of insurance. Life insurance policies are treated as U.S. situs property if issued by a U.S. insurer. If a NRNC owns a U.S. situs policy on the life of another person (even a family member), the value of the policy forms part of the owner's taxable U.S. estate.

---

[98] IRC §2105(a).
[99] *Id. See also* IRC §2105(a).

Estate tax on the value of life insurance held by a NRNC (insuring other people) may be avoided by purchasing the insurance from insurers outside the U.S. This avoids ownership of a taxable U.S. situs asset at death. Alternatively, direct ownership of U.S. life insurance on another person may be avoided by holding the policy in a foreign entity.

> If life insurance is owned by (and benefits) a foreign corporation, neither the cash value nor the payment of proceeds to the owner (upon the death of the insured) creates a taxable event.

This is the case because life insurance proceeds are not subject to income tax[100] and the foreign entity (owning valuable life insurance) has no taxable estate. Please see page 53 below for a discussion on the use of foreign corporations.

---

[100] IRC §101(a)(1).

SHIFTING ASSETS FROM U.S. SITUS

Foreign Corporations

Although lifetime gifts of U.S. intangibles by NRNCs are exempt from Gift Tax, all U.S. situs assets (both tangible and intangible, unless exempt) trigger the Estate Tax upon the death of a NRNC owner. Those same assets held in a foreign corporation are, however, excluded from Estate Tax.[101]

The foreign corporation is used to break the Estate and Gift Tax connection of U.S. situs assets to the foreign individual or trust.

> Shares in a foreign corporation held by a NRNC are considered situated outside the U.S. and subject to neither Gift Tax nor Estate Tax.[101]

---

[101] IRC §2104(a).
[102] Treas. Reg. §20.2105-1(f).

Treasury Regulations indicate that the "situs" of an entity is determined by looking at the place where the entity is created or organized.[103] The regulations further state that this test applies "irrespective of the location of the (ownership) certificates."[104] Consequently, shares of stock owned by the decedent in a U.S. entity are subject to Estate Tax.[105] Conversely, ownership by a NRNC in a foreign corporate entity (if properly organized) is not subject to Estate Tax.[106] The income tax aspects of using an entity taxable as a corporation or partnership should also be carefully considered.

A foreign trust formed by a NRNC to invest in U.S. situs assets should make investments through a foreign holding company, to avoid any potential exposure to the Estate Tax on trust assets. The holding company must carefully comply with

---

[103] Treas. Reg. §20.2104-1(a)(5); §301.7701-5(a).
[104] Treas. Reg. §20.2104-1(a)(5); §20.2105-1(f) (shares of stock issued by a foreign corporation are not U.S. situs assets).
[105] *Id.*
[106] This conclusion is reached because IRC §2104(a) states that shares of stock are treated as having a US "situs" "only if issued by a domestic corporation."

applicable corporate formalities and be treated (for legal, financial and operational purposes) as separate and distinct from its owner(s).

U.S. property transferred by a NRNC to a foreign trust during his or her life remains subject to Estate Tax if the grantor retained at his death the power "to alter, amend, revoke, or terminate" the rights of the beneficiary. [107] If the NRNC grantor may revoke or deplete a foreign trust which owns U.S. situs property, the IRS will include in the NRNC's estate any trust assets in the United States.[108] U.S. assets contributed to a foreign trust by a NRNC grantor (with control over the trust) become subject to Estate Tax upon the grantor's death.

The NRNC grantor of a foreign revocable trust holding U.S. situs property must therefore move trust assets into a foreign holding company (itself owned by the trust) before death. The

---

[107] §2038(a)(1).

[108] §2104(b); *See* <u>Rev. Rul. 55-163</u>, 1955-1 C.B. 674 (situs of equitable interest in conventional private trusts is determined by reference to underlying assets).

foreign corporation will generally break the Estate Tax connection to the NRNC. The NRNC grantor may otherwise reduce the risk of incurring Estate Tax by relinquishing control of (and benefit from) the trust. However, if he or she dies within three years after relinquishing such rights, the Estate Tax will not be avoided.

Foreign trust assets may subject a NRNC grantor to Estate Tax even if trust assets are foreign-situs (on the date of the grantor's death).[109] If U.S. property was initially in the trust but was later sold and replaced with foreign assets, such assets may be deemed U.S. if the transfer occurred within three years of the NRNC's death.[110]

Interestingly, transferring U.S. stock in an existing corporation to a foreign holding company may cause a foreign holding company to be treated as a U.S. corporation for tax

---

[109] IRC §2104(b); 2105.

[110] IRC §2104(b) ("any property of which the decedent has made a transfer, by trust or otherwise, within the meaning of sections 2035 to 2038, inclusive, shall be deemed to be situated in the United States, if so situated either at the time of the transfer or at the time of the decedent's death."

purposes.[111] Until 2017, the 35% U.S. corporate tax rate was one of the highest on earth and applied to worldwide corporate income. Shifting ownership abroad typically reduced net income tax.

The legislative intent of Code §7874(b) is to block the shift of ownership to a low-income tax jurisdiction. Deemed U.S. corporation status (of a foreign holding company) applies if: (i) the U.S. corporation becomes a subsidiary of a foreign corporation or otherwise transfers substantially all its assets to a foreign corporation; (ii) the former shareholders of the U.S. corporation hold at least 80% of the foreign corporation's stock; and (iii) the foreign corporation does not have substantial business activities in the foreign country of incorporation.[112]

Three common corporate inversions (or corporate "expatriations") are as follows. One type is through "substantial activity" or business presence where a U.S. corporation with substantial business activity in a foreign company creates a

---

[111] IRC §7874(b).
[112] *See* H.R. Conf. Rep. No. 108-755, at 560–61 (2004).

foreign subsidiary, and then exchanges stock with it. This is also called a "naked" inversion and does not result in the change of ultimate control of either corporation.

The second is where a U.S. corporation merges with a foreign corporation. The foreign corporation survives, shifting control and operations outside the U.S.

The third inversion is where a U.S. corporation acquires a smaller foreign corporation (to expatriate corporate residence). The U.S. corporation retains control of the newly formed company.

Since 2014, Treasury regulations broaden the regulatory net.[113] Anti-inversion regulations provide that if at least 80% ownership of the new foreign corporation is retained, the offshore entity will be deemed a U.S. corporation and reap no tax benefits of the reorganization. Furthermore, the anti-inversion regulations provide that if the U.S. shareholders retain less than 80% but at least 60% of the new corporation, then the new corporation is not

---

[113] *See* Treasury Notice 2014-52.

deemed a U.S. corporation, but is prohibited from using U.S. tax credits or net operating losses to offset gains from asset transfers to the new corporation. Also, anti-inversion regulations make it harder for U.S. corporations merging or acquiring a foreign corporation to avoid 80% control (by prohibiting certain techniques prior to the merger, such as inflating the size of the foreign entity, shrinking the U.S. corporation, or inverting only a portion of the U.S. entity).

Real Property

Real property has tax situs in the jurisdiction in which it is located. Consequently, U.S. real estate (a tangible asset) is included in the taxable estate of a NRNC.[114]

---

[114] Treas. Reg. §20.2104-1(a)(1).

> If real estate is instead owned by a foreign corporation (itself owned by the NRNC), the property is excluded from Gift Tax and Estate Tax.

The NRNC acquiring U.S. real estate should do so through a foreign corporation. If U.S. real estate is initially purchased directly by the NRNC, the subsequent transfer of the property to an offshore corporation could have tax consequences. Appreciated U.S. real estate held by a NRNC may trigger taxable gain upon transfer to a foreign corporation.[115]

Partnerships

Unlike the rules regarding corporate stock, the tax situs rules for foreign entities taxed as partnerships is ambiguous. The limited case law suggests that a factual examination of the partnership's assets and business activities is necessary to

---

[115] IRC §897(j).

determine the situs of the partnership.[116] The IRS will not rule on exactly how to determine the situs of foreign partnership interests in the hands of a NRNC.[117] Situs may be based on such factors as where the partnership does business or holds assets or where the equity holder resides.

IRS rulings suggest that the taxable estate of an NRNC will include his pro-rata share of U.S. assets held by a foreign partnership if either (i) the country of formation does not recognize the partnership as a legal entity or (ii) the partnership dissolves upon the death of a partner.[118] In either case, the partnership entity is disregarded and its U.S. assets are deemed owned by the partners (and situated in the United States).[119] A U.S. federal appeals court confirmed that dissolution of a foreign entity upon the death of one of its owners causes its U.S. assets to be included in the NRNC owner's estate.[120]

---

[116] See *Blodgett v. Silberman*, 277 U.S. 1 (1928).

[117] Rev. Proc. 2015-7.

[118] STILL CANNOT FIND CITE

[119] *Sanchez v. Bowers*, 70 F.2d 715 (2d Cir.1934).

[120] *See* Rev. Rul. 82-82, 1982-1 C.B. 127, *supra* note 6064 supra.

If the country where the partnership was organized recognizes the partnership as a legal entity (which survives the death of a partner), then equity in the partnership will likely be recognized by the IRS. Situs of equity in the partnership must then be determined.

One court ruled that if equity in a foreign partnership is intangible property, situs is the domicile of the decedent.[121] Treaties (if applicable) typically follow the same logic.

One IRS position is that equity has situs at the business location of the partnership. In any case, the situs of an IRS recognized partnership seems unrelated to the location of partnership property.[122]

If the entity is recognized by the IRS, avoidance of U.S. situs can therefore likely be accomplished by, for example, either, avoiding U.S. operations or holding equity in a foreign corporation. Foreign situs will keep the value of equity outside the U.S. estate of the NRNC partner.

---

[121] See *Blodgett v. Silberman*, 277 U.S. 1 (1928).
[122] Revenue Ruling 55-701., 1955-2 C.B. 836.

The Limited Liability Company

The clarity of U.S. law establishing the country of organization as situs of "corporate" stock, makes foreign limited liability companies ("LLCs") an attractive option. The LLC is generally more protective of owner equity than the corporation. Although LLC membership interests are not identical to corporate stock, Treasury Regulations treat foreign LLCs as corporations for tax purposes (unless the LLC elects otherwise), if all members have limited liability.[123] If any of the members do not have limited liability, the LLC is treated as a tax partnership.[124] Establishing limited liability is typically not difficult.

If a foreign LLC is treated as a corporation for tax purposes, ownership interests in the LLC are not U.S. situs property and may be transferred tax-free by NRNCs (during life

---

[123] Treas. Reg. §301.7701-3(b)(2)(i)(B). Technically, this section classifies an entity as an "association," but Treas. Reg. §301.7701-2(b)(2) makes clear that this designation is akin to being a corporation.
[124] Treas. Reg. §301.7701-3(b)(2)(i)(A).

or at death).[125] One planning technique (discussed on page 59) is to own U.S. real estate (or a U.S. real estate holding company) through a foreign LLC (itself owned by the NRNC or a foreign entity). Such structure moves the situs of ultimate ownership offshore (avoiding Estate and Gift Tax). In the case of appreciated real estate (and other U.S. assets subject to tax on gains from sale), no tax is payable on appreciation until the property itself is sold (irrespective of any transfer of the foreign entity owner).

---

[125] *Pierre v. Commissioner*, 133 T.C. 24 (2009), (holding that although a single-member LLC is disregarded for *income tax* purposes, the entity must be respected for *Gift Tax* purposes when determining whether the assets gifted were the LLC's assets or ownership in the LLC itself).

TREATIES

Double Taxation

People living, investing or doing business in more than one country face exposure to "double" estate and gift tax. This is true because different countries may impose estate or gift tax on the same asset. Two (or more) countries may claim (i) tax situs over the same property or (ii) domicile over the same person (owning taxable property). If two or more countries impose transfer tax on a particular asset or class of assets, tax planning is required.

The U.S. imposes Estate and Gift Tax on its citizens <u>and</u> <u>residents</u>, covering assets held anywhere on earth. See page 3 above. Most other countries tax only persons living within their borders.[126] U.S. citizens living abroad are taxed worldwide by the U.S. and (potentially) by the country of domicile. Non-citizens

---

[126] For example, a U.S. citizen with assets in the U.S. and Cuba is subject to U.S. Estate and Gift Tax on all assets (both in Cuba and the U.S.). A Cuban national (living in Cuba) with assets in Cuba and the U.S. subjects only assets in Cuba to Cuban estate and gift tax (leaving the IRS to tax the U.S. situs assets).

living in the U.S. similarly face potential double Estate and Gift Tax, by the U.S. and their home country. See pages 5-7. Double taxation of U.S. citizens and residents may arise in a variety of scenarios, including the following:

o The U.S. imposes tax on the basis of U.S. citizenship and another country taxes on the basis of a different domicile or residence (for example, U.S. citizens residing outside the U.S.);

o The reverse, where a foreign nation taxes all assets of a deceased foreign national (based on citizenship) and the U.S. taxes all such assets based on the deceased's U.S. domicile at death;

o The U.S. and the other country both impose tax on the basis of citizenship when the decedent has dual citizenship;

o The U.S. taxes based on the situs of assets (within the U.S.) and the other country taxes the assets on the basis of domicile or relationship of the decedent to the foreign nation;

o The foreign country imposes tax on the basis of the situs of assets (in that country) and the U.S. taxes the same assets based on the U.S. domicile or citizenship of the decedent;

o Two decedents may be taxed on the same asset if one country taxes the (resident or citizen) owner and another taxes the (resident or citizen) beneficiary (of the same asset).

Foreign Estate Tax Credit

In the absence of a treaty, the Code may provide a U.S. Estate Tax credit, to the extent of estate tax (or any similar succession tax) paid to a foreign country on property also taxed by the U.S.[127]

---

[127] IRC §2014(a).

There is no similar U.S. tax credit for gift tax paid abroad. Gift tax treaties, do, however, provide for the credit. See page 9.

If an estate tax treaty applies, double tax may be avoided by utilizing the foreign tax credit available either under the treaty or under the Code. If a treaty position is taken on a U.S. tax return, Form 8833, *Treaty-Based Return Position Disclosure Under Section 6114, or 7701(b)*, may be required.[128] U.S. residents, citizens and investors must plan to insure that a tax credit is available to cover any estate or gift tax paid to a foreign nation.

Treaties Generally

U.S. Estate and Gift Tax treaties are intended to prevent double taxation by the U.S. and another country (of the same property).

---

[128] §6114 and §6712; Reg. §301.6114-1.

> Treaties generally eliminate double taxation for both (i) NRNC decedents dying with U.S. assets[129] and (ii) U.S. citizens and residents with foreign assets.

As noted, U.S. citizens or residents are generally credited (against U.S. Estate and Gift Tax) for estate or gift tax paid abroad. Foreign nationals with U.S. property are generally credited by their home country for U.S. Estate and Gift Tax incurred. The benefit of tax credits may, however, be more limited than the tax savings offered by a treaty.

Specifically, estate tax treaties determine: (a) domicile of the individual taxpayer; (b) tax situs of certain assets; (c) property taxable by the country not of domicile or citizenship; (d) available exemptions, deductions, and credits; (e) how foreign tax credits are applied; (f) rights of estates to negotiate tax problems with

---

[129] IRC §2102(c)(3)(A) governs the unified credit available to NRNCs under treaties and was amended by the Small Business Job Protection Act of 1996, P.L., 104-188, §1704(f)(1), effective Aug. 20, 1996.

treaty partners; and (g) financial information exchanged by treaty nations.[130]

Dual residents are assigned a single nation of residence by the applicable treaty (typically the country with closer ties to the individual). Additionally, to benefit from situs-type estate tax treaties, a decedent must have a personal affiliation, such as domicile or citizenship, with at least one treaty country.

As of March 2019, the U.S. has in force the following treaties governing the Estate Tax, Gift Tax or both.

Estate and Gift Tax Treaties:

Australia

Austria

Denmark

France

Germany

---

[130] *See, e.g.,* U.S.-Australia Treaty; *See* Jeffrey A. Schoenblum, U.S. Estate and Gift Tax Transfers, BNA Tax Management Portfolio No. 851 – 2nd, 1, 1 (2019).

Japan

United Kingdom

Estate Tax Treaties:[131]

Finland

Greece

Ireland

Italy

Netherlands

Norway

South Africa

Switzerland

---

[131] Since 1972, Canada has no estate tax and instead imposes an income tax on capital gains from a deemed disposition of property at death. Therefore, the U.S. and Canada do not have an Estate Tax Treaty, but rather handle functional "death tax" matters under the 1995 Protocol Amending the Convention Between the United States of America and Canada with Respect to Taxes on Income and Capital, Mar. 17, 1995 (hereinafter "1995 U.S.-Canada Protocol").

Gift Tax Treaties:[132]

Australia

Austria

Denmark

France

Germany

Japan

United Kingdom

Estate and gift tax treaties avoid double taxation pursuant to either a situs or domicile format. The country of applicable situs or domicile is afforded the right to impose estate or gift tax on the individual. Situs treaties establish assets as inside the

---

[132] These Gift Tax Treaties may be combined with Estate Tax Treaties. Canada imposes no gift tax, yet lifetime dispositions of appreciated property will generate a capital gains tax. *See* Jonah Ravel, *Cross-border Gift Tax Issues for Canadians: Tips to avoid double taxation and other strategies*, ADVISOR'S EDGE (Feb. 8, 2019), https://www.advisor.ca/tax/tax-news/cross-border-gift-tax-issues-for-canadians/.

borders of (and taxable by) only one treaty partner. Domicile treaties deem the relevant person as domiciled in (and taxed by) only one treaty country. In general, treaties established prior to 1970 are situs-based. Later treaties are generally domicile-based. The fifteen existing U.S. estate tax treaties (broken-down by type) are as follows:

Situs	Domicile
Australia	Austria
Finland	Canada
Greece	Denmark
Ireland	France
Italy	Germany
Japan	Netherlands
South Africa	Switzerland
	United Kingdom

Situs Treaties

Situs treaties allow citizens and residents of treaty countries to avoid double taxation on particular classes of property.

> Situs treaties establish the situs of assets and assign taxing authority (over such assets) to the situs country.

Planning should make clear which country has situs to assets (pursuant to the treaty). Once situs is clear, the country with situs may impose estate tax (and the other country provides a credit for such tax against any estate tax it would otherwise impose). This avoids double taxation.

The following example may be helpful in understanding how double taxation occurs, based on differing definitions of situs. Consider an NRNC with stock in a U.S. corporation, certificates for which are held in a non-treaty country. U.S. tax law places situs in the U.S. (the country of incorporation). The foreign country where the share certificates are located may also impose estate tax on the value of the shares. The NRNC would receive no U.S. tax credit for the foreign tax imposed on the shares because the U.S. does not recognize the foreign tax situs of the shares. The stock would therefore be subject to double estate tax upon the death of the owner.

Situs treaties (limiting situs to a single country) eliminate the imposition of estate tax by two countries on the same property. The situs treaty permits only one country to tax a particular asset based on an agreed situs of (in our example) the corporate stock. If agreed situs is (for example) the location of the certificates, the U.S. would credit the NRNC against U.S. Estate Tax for the amount of foreign estate tax paid on the shares to the situs country.[133] The treaty benefits only apply to domiciliaries or citizens of either the U.S. or a treaty partner.

One additional complexity is that the treaty country without situs (over a particular asset) may still tax the asset based

---

[133] *See* Schoenblum, *supra* note 110, at 5-6 (explaining that a country which taxes based on personal affiliation such as domicile "must allow a credit under a situs-type treaty for the tax imposed by the situs country.").

on the "personal affiliation" of the decedent, beneficiary, grantor or grantee (to the non-situs country). Thus, one country may tax an estate asset based on situs (established by treaty) and the other may tax the same asset based on the owner's affiliation to that country. The personal affiliation (triggering double taxation) is typically domicile, residence or citizenship. Double taxation of the particular asset (based on personal affiliation) may be reduced by a treaty requirement that the affiliated country (without situs) credit (against its estate tax) the affiliated individual for the tax imposed by the situs country.[134] Without such particular treaty language, the country of domicile or "affiliation" could deny any tax credit against estate tax imposed by the affiliated country.[135]

The following is an example of how a situs treaty may eliminate double taxation based on personal affiliation. An Argentine citizen domiciled in Miami with real estate in Australia

---

[134] *Id.* As aforementioned, Canada had a 1962 situs treaty with the U.S. until the enactment of the 1995 U.S.-Canada Protocol.

[135] Generally, situs-type treaties are limited to death or estate taxes, with the exception of Japan, which has a situs treaty with the U.S. with respect to gift taxes. *See Id.* at 6.

is subject (upon his death) to Australian estate tax on such real estate. The U.S. also imposes estate tax on the real estate (and all other property of the Argentine) based on his U.S. domicile. Pursuant to the U.S./Australia treaty, the U.S. will credit the Argentine's U.S. Estate Tax (dollar-for-dollar tax) by the amount of (situs-based) estate tax imposed by Australia.

Note that Argentina imposes estate tax on the worldwide assets of its citizens. In light of the absence of a treaty between Argentina and Australia, Argentina may not offer a credit against estate tax paid in Australia.

Our Argentine national could return permanently to Argentina but retain ownership of stock in a U.S. corporation. The stock is deemed by the United States to have a situs in the United States. If the stock certificates are held in Japan, the asset is deemed by Japan to have a situs in Japan. Even though the treaty between the United States and Japan specifies that the situs of corporate stock is the location of stock certificates, the treaty does not apply. The situs treaty requires the decedent to have a relationship (domicile/residence/citizen) with either treaty country i.e., Japan or U.S.

The application of a tax credit is therefore conditioned on the decedent being a citizen or domiciliary of either the United States or Japan.[136] The U.S., Japan and Argentina may therefore all impose estate tax on the shares (with no means of relief from double (or triple) taxation). The foreign tax credit available under Internal Revenue Code (§2014 for Estate Tax paid abroad) is also not available, because the United States deems the stock to have a U.S. situs (making a credit for situs-based tax paid abroad unavailable).

Situs-type treaties primarily apply to the Estate Tax. The U.S./Japan (situs) treaty is the only situs treaty also covering gift tax.[137] The U.S. does not otherwise credit U.S. domiciliaries for gift tax paid abroad (against U.S. Gift Tax paid to the IRS on the same gifts).

---

[136] U.S.-Japan Treaty art. V(1) suggests that the country of domicile or other personal affiliation will grant an estate the tax credit, leaving the situs country to collect estate tax.
[137] U.S.-Japan Treaty art. I(1)(a),(b).

The double taxation of gifts by resident aliens (RAs) and NRNCs is an open exposure. Also, certain assets, such as bank accounts, are not covered by several existing situs treaties.[138] Moreover, the situs of certain assets, such as rights to real estate and equity in hybrid business entities (like LLCs), may (depending on the treaty) be unclear.

Domicile Treaties

Double taxation often arises from investment or residency in foreign countries.

> Domicile-based Estate and Gift Tax treaties generally resolve the issue of double taxation by permitting the country of domicile to tax the entire estate of the deceased (on a worldwide basis).

---

[138] Treaties with Australia, Japan (U.S.-Japan Treat art. III(1)(c), and Greece (U.S.-Greece Treat art. IV(2)(j) provide for the situs of bank accounts (as located in the country of domicile or residence of the decedent) and define bank accounts and the rights associated with them, whereas other situs treaties do not so provide.

The non-domicile country may only tax certain classes of assets.[139] For example, under the U.S.-Austria Treat art. 5(2), the non-domiciliary country may tax only real estate or property associated with a fixed place of business (in that country).

The key is to clearly establish "fiscal domicile" in a single country (assigned tax jurisdiction). The "fiscal domicile" is typically where the individual has a "closer connection" to the governing country.[140] To qualify for the benefits of a domicile-based estate/gift tax treaty, the decedent/grantor must be domiciled in a treaty nation at the time of the death or gift. If the

---

[139] The non-domicile country agreeing to a domicile treaty will agree to not exercise jurisdiction to tax certain situs assets, except when a property is "so connected to a country and under its control that the traditional primacy of situs taxation is preserved with respect to such property." *See* Schoenblum, at 83.

[140] *See, e.g.*, Rev. Rul. 82-82, 1982-1 C.B. 127. By art. XXX(8) of the Convention Between the United States of America and Canada with Respect to Taxes on Income and on Capital, Sept. 26, 1980, T.I.A.S. 11087 (hereafter "U.S.-Canada Income Tax Treaty") which entered into force Aug. 16, 1984, the U.S.-Canada Estate Tax Treaty terminated effective for decedents dying on or after Jan. 1, 1985.

nation competing with the U.S. for domicile is not party to a treaty

with the U.S., double taxation is a concern.

For example, if a French citizen and resident gifts U.S.

tangible property to a child in France, the Code taxes the transfer.

However, the U.S.-France Treaty assigns exclusive taxing

jurisdiction to France.[141] Interestingly, if France does not impose

tax on the transfer, the IRS may not impose tax (even though U.S.

property was gifted).

The nation of citizenship may also claim tax

authority.[142] The definition of domicile (establishing the treaty

partner with taxing authority) may differ even among treaty

partners. The U.S. Treasury model tax treaty establishes domicile

under the domestic law of each treaty nation.[143] To avoid an

---

[141] U.S.-France Treaty art. 7(1) (except to the extent taxed by the other treaty country under the "permanent establishment rules," the suits state may tax such property, and if the property is *in transitu*, it is taxed at the destination).

[142] *See, e.g.,* references to citizenship as the determinative personal affiliation for discerning fiscal domicile in U.S.-Denmark Treaty art. 4.3; U.S.-Germany Treaty (as amended by a 1998 Protocol), art. 4(3); and U.S.-Austria Treaty art. 4(3).

[143] *See* U.S. Model Tax Treaty art. 4.

individual being conserved a dual domiciliary, the model treaty contains a tie-breaking provision establishing a single domicile country.

A credit is necessary (to avoid double taxation) if (for example) the U.S. taxes based on citizenship and the other treaty country taxes based of domicile. Under domicile treaties, if one treaty country (i.e., the U.S.) taxes assets of its citizens worldwide, it will credit (against its tax) the tax imposed by the country of domicile.[144]

The definition of domicile may differ among countries. Certain domicile treaties establish a single definition of "fiscal domicile" (to avoid more than one nation claiming estate or gift tax domicile over the same person).[145] Where the U.S. and a foreign nation claim domicile (and estate tax) over one person,

---

[144] IRC §2102.
[145] *See, e.g.*, U.S.-Germany Treaty; art. 4(1)(a)-(b) (Germany defines fiscal domicile as either a domicile or habitual abode); U.S.-France Treaty art. 4(2)(a)-(e) (each country's domestic laws determine the definition of fiscal domicile and if that determination is insufficient to discern taxing authority, the countries apply a hierarchy of personal affiliations to determine which one has domicile).

treaties with Austria, Denmark, France, Netherlands, United Kingdom and Germany establish a single domicile.[146]

If Australia, Finland, Greece, Ireland, Japan, South Africa, or Switzerland dispute domicile with the U.S., the treaties leave the determination of domicile to the laws of the treaty partners (which may not coincide).[147] If two treaty countries claim fiscal domicile, the following factors typically apply to determine proper domicile:

• where the person maintained a "permanent home";

• the country with the closest personal relation (center of vital interests);

• the "habitual abode"; and

• the country of citizenship.

---

[146] *See* U.S.-U.K. Treaty art. 4(1)(a)-(b); U.S.-Netherlands Treaty art. 4(1)-(2); U.S.-Germany Treaty art. 4(1)-(2); U.S.-France Treaty art. 4(1)-(2); U.S.-Denmark Treaty art. 4.1(a)-(b); U.S.-Austria Treaty art. 4(1)-(2).
[147] *See* U.S.-South Africa Treaty art. III(1); U.S.-Japan Treaty art. II(3); U.S.-Greece Treaty art. IV(1); U.S.-Australia Treaty art. II(3).

If neither treaty nation can clearly establish these personal affiliations, the countries must work out an agreement on fiscal domicile.[148]

> Although domicile treaties afford exclusive taxing authority to the country of fiscal domicile, certain assets (with a strong connection to one situs) may be excluded.

Real estate, business property (at a permanent establishment) and a fixed foreign base for performance of personal services, may be taxed by the situs nation.[149] In such case, the domicile country will allow a credit for tax by the situs treaty partner. All other assets are taxable exclusively by the domicile country. An Estate or Gift Tax credit (by the domicile country for tax paid in the situs country) is therefore only necessary to avoid double taxation on

---

[148] *See, e.g.,* U.S.-Germany Treaty art. II(5) (where fiscal domicile changes over time and each country's test still results in double taxation, each treaty country can form agreements as to certain credits or refunds).

[149] *See* U.S.-Austria Treaty art. 5(1) (real property can be taxed by the situs country); *id.* art. 6(1) (business property can be taxed by the situs country).

certain classes of property (as all other property may only be taxed by the domicile country).

The exceptions to domicile-based taxation (permitting the taxation of certain assets situated in the non-domicile country) can (as with situs treaties) raise the issue of differing definitions of asset situs. Where situs is disputed, double taxation is possible.

Consider a U.S. resident (non-citizen) who owns a business enterprise in a domicile treaty country. The treaty nation partner may claim that the operation is a "permanent establishment" inside the treaty partner. The treaty will allow the nation of business establishment to tax the business assets, even if it is not the fiscal domicile of the decedent. The typical problem is that the U.S. may deem the business assets as U.S. situs (owned by the resident non-citizen), even if the assets are not in the U.S. In such case, the U.S. provides no credit for tax paid abroad. A treaty may resolve the issue but often fails to provide a clear answer. [150]   The problem is not that a permanent business establishment exists, but that the treaty countries disagree as to its situs.

Although one country may tax a lifetime gift, a different (non-treaty) country may impose estate tax on the same asset. Only by treaty may the gift tax be credited against the later death tax. Only a few treaties resolve the issue.[151] For example, Article 11.5 of the U.S.-Germany Treaty provides that the crediting treaty partner "take into account in an appropriate way" to credit tax on a prior gift by the other treaty country if the property is taxed by the crediting country at death.[152]

---

[150] *See* U.S.-Austria Treaty art. 7(2) (which lacks a clear definition of whether a property right is real property or businesses property; the treaty says that the law of the non-domiciliary treaty country will govern instead of providing a clear answer).

[151] All U.S. domicile-type treaties (except the treaty with the Netherlands) apply to gifts and estates, but generally, fail to credit gift tax paid against estate tax. Situs-type treaties (assigning tax situs to different classes of property), similarly, make no reference to adjustment of estate tax for tax paid on lifetime gifts, with the exception of the U.S.-Japan situs treaty.

[152] Regs. §20.0-1(b)-1)-estate tax); §2501(a)(1) and Regs. §§25.2511-1(b), -3(a)(1) (gift tax).

The IRS requires notice of a treaty-based tax position.[153]

Taxpayers seeking treaty benefits must file Form 8833, Treaty-Based Return Position Disclosure, under Section 6114 or 7701(b), to take a treaty-based return position. Dual-resident taxpayers use this form to make the treaty-based return position disclosure required by Treasury Regulations §§301.7701(b)-7.

---

[153] IRC §6114.

EXCHANGE OF TAX INFORMATION

Treaties

The IRS exchanges tax information with other countries pursuant to both situs and domicile tax treaties.[154] A broad range of Estate Tax and related information is exchanged "as is necessary ... for the prevention of fraud or the administration of statutory provisions against tax avoidance ... ."[155] Information may be exchanged involving a decedent, related family and entities. Information may be related to any tax investigation or attempt to avoid Estate or Gift Tax. Any tax information legally available (under the tax law of the contracting states) may be exchanged.[156]

---

[154] *See, e.g.,* U.S.-Austria Treaty art. 12 (domicile tax treaty) and U.S.-Greece Treaty (situs tax treaty).

[155] U.S.-Finland Treaty art. VII.

[156] *See, e.g.,* U.S.-Germany Treaty, art. 14; *See generally U.S. v. Powell*, 379 U.S. 48, 57-58 (1964). The test for relevance is whether the summons seeks information "which might throw light upon the correctness of the taxpayer's return." *U.S. v. Cox*, 73 F. Supp.2d 751, 758 (S.D. Tex. 1999).

The IRS generally has three forms of information exchange. The first, "spontaneous" information exchanges, transfers certain tax information without request. The information provided may, for example, arise from an investigation which is likely of interest to the treaty partner. The U.S. engages in spontaneous exchange of information with almost all treaty countries.[157]

The second, "routine" exchanges, are also known as "automatic exchanges of information." Disclosure generally involves income tax return processing. Foreign partners agree to exchange certain tax or financial account-related information on a regular and systematic basis, without the need for a specific request, pursuant to a tax treaty or tax information exchange agreement. [158]

The third, "special" requests for information, are made on a case-by-case basis.[159]

---

[157] *See, e.g.,* U.S.-Austria Treaty art. 12(1).
[158] IRM 4.60.1.4 (09-19-14).
[159] IRM 4.60.1.2 (09-19-14) (these exchanges are described as "specific exchanges of information").

U.S. exchange requests with (foreign tax agencies) are administered by the Program Manager(s) of the Exchange of Information in Washington, DC ("EOI HQ"); the Revenue Service Representative ("RSR") in Plantation, Florida; the overseas Tax Attaché; or the Program Manager of the Joint International Tax Shelter Information Centre ("JITSIC") in Washington, DC.[160]

To obtain information, the IRS may issue an Information Document Request Form 4564.[161] If the response is inadequate or untimely, the IRS[162] may then issue a Formal Document Request (FDR), a presummons letter or a summons pursuant to Section 7602 of the Code.[163] If the request is not honored or a petition to quash is filed, the IRS may seek enforcement, after review by Associate Chief Counsel (International), in conjunction with the

---

[160] IRM 4.60.1.2.1(1), (2) (09-19-14), IRM 4.60.1.2.2(1) (09-19-14).
[161] IRM 4.61.2.2 (5-1-06).
[162] IRM Exhibit 4.46.1-1 (7-22-11), IRM 4.46.4.4.2 (3-1-06), IRM 4.61.2.4 (5-1-06), IRM 35.4.5.2.1 (8-11-04). *See generally* IRM 1.2.43.12 (7-1-10).
[163] IRM 4.61.2.4 (5-01-06).

Tax Division of the Justice Department. [164] To enforce a summons, the IRS must prove its good faith investigation. [165]

> No statute of limitations restricts the exchange of information. Tax information may therefore be exchanged even if the underlying tax claim cannot be pursued (because too much time has passed).

Tax Information Exchange Agreements

The U.S. and several non-treaty partners have also agreed to share tax information.

---

[164] IRM 34.6.3.6.6(3), (4) (2-1-11).
[165] *See U.S. v. Stuart*, 489 U.S. 353, 356 (1989); See IRM 34.63.6 6 – "Tax Treaty and TIEA Summonses" (02-01-11).

> Tax Information Exchange Agreements ("TIEAs") allow for information sharing with countries with which the U.S. does not have an income tax treaty.

The U.S. entered into its first TIEA in 1984 with Barbados (the first U.S. tax information exchange arrangement with a non-treaty partner).[166]

The U.S. has signed the following Tax Information Exchange Agreements:

American Samoa

Antigua & Barbuda

Argentina

Aruba

Bahamas

Barbados

---

[166] *See* Second Protocol Amending the Convention Between the United States of America and Barbados for the Avoidance of Double Taxation and the Prevention of Fiscal Evasion with respect to Taxes on Income signed on December 31, 1984 (effective July 14, 2004) (hereinafter "U.S.-Barbados TIEA").

Bermuda

Bonaire, Sint Eustatius, & Saba

Brazil

British Virgin Islands

Cayman Islands

Colombia

Costa Rica

Curaçao

Dominica

Dominican Republic

Gibraltar

Grenada

Guernsey

Guyana

Honduras

Hong Kong

Isle of Man

Jamaica

Jersey

Liechtenstein

Marshall Islands

Mauritius

Mexico

Monaco

Netherlands Antilles

Panama

Peru

Saint Maarten

St. Lucia

Trinidad & Tobago

The U.S. also has tax information sharing agreements with U.S. possessions. The U.S. offers tax incentives to U.S. possessions to sign tax exchange agreements.

The U.S. Virgin Islands has entered into a "Working Arrangement to deem a return filed with the Virgin Islands by a bona fide resident of the Virgin Islands as a U.S. income tax return,"[167] provided that the U.S. and the Virgin Islands have entered into an agreement for the routine exchange of income tax information satisfying the requirements of the IRS Commissioner.[168] The U.S. also has tax coordination agreements (for information tax exchange and mutual assistance to prevent evasion) with American Samoa, Guam, the Commonwealth of the Northern Mariana Islands, Puerto Rico, and the U.S. Virgin Islands.[169]

The Caribbean Basin Economic Recovery Act of 1983 (CBERA) (also known as the "Caribbean Basin Initiative") also provides certain benefits to countries that exchange tax

---

[167] *See* Tax Implementation Agreement Between the U.S. and the Virgin Islands (effective Feb. 24, 1987).

[168] Internal Revenue Cumulative Bulletin 2008-1 page 958.

[169] *See* Tax Coordination Agreement Between the United States of America and the Commonwealth of the Northern Mariana Islands (effective Jan. 30, 2003), Agreement on Coordination of Tax Administration between the United States of America and Guam (effective July 12, 1985), Tax Coordination Agreement Between the United States of America and the Commonwealth of Puerto Rico (effective May 26, 1989), Tax Implementation Agreement Between the United States of America and American Samoa (effective Jan. 1, 1988), Tax Implementation Agreement Between the United States of America and the U.S. Virgin islands (effective Feb. 24, 1987).

information with the IRS.[170] As part of the Caribbean Basin Initiative, Section 274(h) was added to the Code.

> Section 274(h) generally restricts U.S. income tax deductions for expenses related to a convention, seminar, or similar meeting held outside the "North American area."

The "North American area" includes the United States, its possessions, the Trust Territory of the Pacific Islands, Canada and Mexico. Certain Caribbean countries and Bermuda, which have signed a tax information exchange agreement, are also treated as part of the North American area.[171]

---

[170] Pub. L. No. 98-67, §201–§231, 19 USC §2701–§2707. The Act provides three specific benefits to countries agreeing to exchange tax information. First, the Act makes deductible in the U.S. (Code §274(h)) the costs of hosting conventions, business meetings and seminars. Second, the costs of hosting a foreign sales corporation (as defined in former Code §922) are deductible. Lastly, participating nations may receive loans qualifying for benefits under former Code §936.
[171] IRC §274(h); §274 defines "beneficiary" country to include countries covered by §212(a)(1)(A) of the Caribbean Basin Economic Recovery Act and Bermuda (CBERA), but does not include some later contracting countries with TIEAs such as Peru.

Specifically, the North American area [172] includes the following:

The 50 United States and District of Columbia;

U.S. Possessions: American Samoa, Baker Island, the Commonwealth of Puerto Rico, the Commonwealth of the Northern Mariana Islands, Guam, Howland Island, Jarvis Island, Johnston Island, Kingman Reef, the Midway Islands, Palmyra Atoll, the U.S. Virgin Islands, Wake Island, and other U.S. islands, cays, and reefs not part of the 50 states or the District of Columbia;

Canada,

Mexico,

The Marshall Islands,

Micronesia, and

Palau.

---

[172] Rev. Rul. 2016-16, 2016-26 I.R.B. 1062.

Also included within the North American area are the following countries with which the U.S. has entered into a TIEA that meet certain statutory requirements.[173]

Jurisdiction	Effective Date
Antigua and Barbuda	February 10, 2003
Argentina	December 23, 2016
Aruba	September 13, 2004
Bahamas	January 1, 2004
Barbados	November 3, 1984
Bermuda	December 2, 1988
Bonaire, Sint Eustatius, and Saba	March 22, 2007
Brazil	March 19, 2013
British Virgin Islands	March 10, 2006
Cayman Islands	April 14, 2014
Colombia	April 30, 2014
Costa Rica	February 12, 1991

---

[173] Rev. Rul. 2016-16 (This ruling contains an updated list of all geographical areas included in the North American area for purposes of Section 274 of the Code. Rev. Rul. 2011-26 modified and superseded.).

Curaçao	March 22, 2007
Dominica	May 9, 1988
Dominican Republic	October 12, 1989
Gibraltar	December 22, 2009
Grenada	July 13, 1987
Guernsey	January 1, 2006
Guyana	August 27, 1992
Honduras	October 11, 1991
Hong Kong	June 20, 2014
Isle of Man	January 1, 2004
Jamaica	December 18, 1986
Jersey	June 26, 2006
Liechtenstein	January 1, 2009
Mauritius	August 29, 2014
Monaco	March 11, 2010
Panama	April 18, 2011
Peru	March 31, 1993
Saint Lucia	April 22, 1991

Sint Mauritius	March 22, 2007
Trinidad & Tobago	February 9, 1990

CBERA Sections 212(a)(1)(A) and (B) designate the following countries as "beneficiary countries" entitled to additional tax preferences for conventions and conferences: Anguilla, Antigua and Barbuda, Bahamas, Barbados, Belize, Bermuda, Dominica, Grenada, Guyana, Haiti, Jamaica, Saint Lucia, Saint Vincent and the Grenadines, Surinam, Trinidad and Tobago, Cayman Islands, Montserrat, Netherlands Antilles, St. Kitts and Nevis, Turks and Caicos Islands, and the British Virgin Islands.[174]

Note that entering a tax information agreement does not guarantee an eligible beneficiary country to be included in the "North American area." The tax information exchange must be coordinated with and designated as a CBERA beneficiary country.

---

[174] *See also*, 19 U.S.C. §2702(a)&(b).

Collection of U.S. Tax Abroad

The U.S. cannot generally force another country to collect an IRS debt.

> One country is not required to take action to collect tax owed to a foreign country.[176]

Situs treaties, however, typically permit each country to collect tax covered by the treaty.[176] Domicile treaties do not address or alter the general rule that neither country may force the other to collect tax.

Practically speaking, cooperation among (even situs treaty) countries is necessary. Typically, the country attempting

---

[175] *See, e.g., Moore v. Mitchell*, 30 F.2d 600 (2d Cir. 1929), *aff'd on other grounds*, 281 U.S. 18 (1930); Her Majesty Queen in Right of British Columbia v. Gilbertson, 597 F2d 1161, 1164 (th Cir. 1979) ("[a]pparently … the first time … that a foreign nation has sought enforcement of a tax judgment in a court of the United States"); *U.S. v. Boots*, 80 F.3d 580, 587 (1st Cir. 1996).

[176] *See, e.g.*, U.S.-Finland Treaty art. VIII.

to enforce collection must seek assistance from the treaty partner to collect assets inside the borders of the partner nation.[177]

---

[177] The 2003 OECD Model Income Tax Convention added Article 27 "Assistance in the Collection of Taxes" Article 27(1) and (2) provide that the Contracting States shall lend assistance to each other in the collection of revenue claims.

FOREIGN TRUSTS

Income Tax

Generally

A foreign trust is generally treated as a NRNC for U.S. income tax purposes. Foreign trusts are therefore subject to U.S. income tax only on U.S. source income.[178] Trust distributions to U.S. citizens and income tax residents carry out taxable "distributable net income" to the beneficiary.[179] Additional tax may be recognized for accumulated income, unless the trust qualifies as a "grantor trust." Grantor trusts (generally controlled by the founder) are ignored for income tax purposes.

> Grantor trust assets are deemed owned by the grantor[181] with all U.S. income taxed to the grantor.

---

[178] IRC §§641(b), 872(a).
[179] IRC §§661-662.
[180] IRC §§671-679.

Income Tax Consequences of Creation and Funding by U.S. Persons

Understanding the tax impact on U.S. citizens and U.S. resident grantors and beneficiaries of foreign trusts is helpful to understand the corresponding impact on NRNCs. There are no income tax consequences for a U.S. citizen or resident upon creating a foreign trust. Under certain circumstances, income tax may be imposed on the transfer of property to the foreign trust.

> Internal Revenue Code §684 generally treats the gratuitous transfer of property by a U.S. person to a foreign trust (with no U.S. beneficiary) as a sale or exchange of the assets contributed.

The grantor is deemed to sell the assets transferred for fair market value, triggering taxable gain (but not loss) on the excess of fair market value over tax basis in the transferred property.

The §684 deemed sale of trust assets does not, however, apply to "grantor" trusts (disregarded for income tax purposes, with trust assets deemed owned by the grantor).

> If a foreign trust has a U.S. beneficiary, Code §679 deems the trust a grantor trust. The funding of a foreign trust by a U.S. citizen or resident grantor, for any U.S. beneficiary (including himself), therefore has no immediate U.S. income tax implications.

Grantor status ends upon the earlier of (1) the foreign trust no longer having a U.S. beneficiary or (2) the death of the grantor.[181] In determining whether fair market value is received, if the transferor is the grantor or a trust beneficiary (or a related person within the meaning of I.R.C. §643(i)(2)(B)), any obligation issued by the trust to the transferor (or by certain related persons) is generally disregarded (and treated as a gift of the assets transferred).[182]

---

[181] Treas. Reg. §§1.684-2(e) (death of grantor), §1.679-2(c)(2) (no. U.S. beneficiary for foreign trust).

[182] See I.R.C. §679(a)(3)(A)(i); See also Treas. Reg. §1.679-4(d) providing that certain "qualified obligations" (generally any bond, note, debenture, certificate, bill receivable, account receivable, note

Transfers by U.S. persons to entities owned by a foreign trust are treated as transfers to the foreign trust (followed by a transfer of the asset by the trust to the controlled entity).[183] The deemed funding applies unless the U.S. contributor is not related to a trust beneficiary or proves that the transfer is attributable to his independent ownership in the entity. For example, if a foreign trust and a U.S. contributor jointly fund a corporation, each taking back stock proportionate to their transfers, the funding is not gratuitous and Code §679 is not applicable.

---

receivable, open account, or other evidence of indebtedness, and to the extent not previously described, any annuity contract as defined under Notice 97-34, IRB 1997-25 and I.R.C. §6048) will be recognized as consideration.

[183] Treas. Reg. §1.679-3(f).

Income Tax Treatment Upon Death of U.S. Grantor

Upon the death of the U.S. settlor (resident or citizen) of a foreign grantor trust, grantor status terminates.[184] Death of the grantor triggers two possible tax outcomes.[185] If trust assets are not includable in the gross estate of the U.S. grantor, they are subject to a deemed sale under Code §684 (deemed as transferred to the foreign trust immediately prior to U.S. grantor's death).[186] Following the deemed sale, trust assets receive a basis step-up, based on the recognized gain (but no loss).[187]

> Foreign trust assets includable in the U.S. grantor's gross estate are not subject to deemed sale under Code §684 upon the grantor's death.

---

[184] Treas. Reg. §1.684-2(e).
[185] I.R.C. §684(c); Treas. Reg. §1.684-3(c)(1); Treas. Reg. §1.684-2(e).
[186] I.R.C. §684(c).
[187] Treas. Reg. §1.684-1(a)(2).

Instead, trust assets (which avoid the deemed sale) are subject to Estate Tax and receive a fair market value step-up in basis on the grantor's death.[188] See p. 6 above.

After trust assets are deemed sold or subject to Estate Tax, the trust is treated as an independent foreign non-grantor trust for federal income tax purposes.

Income Taxation of Foreign Trusts Created by NRNC

As a general rule, non-grantor foreign trusts incur taxable income like NRNC individuals (with certain limitations on credits and deductions, unique to trusts).[189] Neither Code §684(a) (deemed sales provisions) nor Code §679 (deemed grantor status) apply to transfers by a NRNC to a foreign trust (with no U.S. beneficiaries). U.S. source income is generally treated (for U.S. income tax purposes) as earned by the foreign non-grantor trust.[190]

---

[188] Treas. Reg. §1.684-3(c)(1).
[189] I.R.C. §§641(b), §872(a). See I.R.C. §§642, 643, 651, and 661 regarding special rules for credits and deductions for trusts.
[190] Unless I.R.C. §672(f) (grantor status) applies to the trust.

U.S. gross income of a foreign non-grantor trust consists only of (1) income derived from sources within the U.S. (not effectively connected with the conduct of a trade or business in the U.S.), and (2) income effectively connected with the conduct of a trade or business within the U.S.[191]

Accordingly, foreign non-grantor trusts are subject to U.S. income tax on the following types of income:

i.   Income Effectively Connected with a U.S. Trade or Business.[192]

ii.   Disposition of U.S. Real Property Interests.[193]

iii.   Fixed or determinable annual or periodic income ("FDAPI") from U.S. sources (interest, dividends, rents, annuities, etc.).[194]

---

[191] See IRC §872(a).
[192] IRC §871(b).
[193] IRC §897(a).
[194] IRC §871(a).

If a NRNC funds a trust for the benefit of a U.S. person, the trust will be treated as a <u>grantor trust as to the U.S. beneficiary</u> (for that portion of the trust benefitting the U.S. beneficiary).[195] The U.S. beneficiary is taxed on worldwide income earned by that portion of trust assets.[196] To avoid having U.S. beneficiaries recognize taxable income and any tax on accumulated income), NRNCs should generally attempt to organize foreign trusts as grantor trusts. In such event, the NRNC grantor is responsible for all U.S. source income recognized by the foreign trust. Since 1996, NRNCs are, however, subject to certain restrictions on establishing a foreign grantor trust.[197] There are three exceptions to non-grantor status of foreign trusts formed by a NRNC:

1.   The Grantor has full power to revoke the trust without the consent of any person, or with the consent of a subservient third-party.[198]

---

[195] Treas. Reg. §1.672(f)-1.
[196] Treas. Reg. §1.671-3.
[197] *See* IRC §672(f).
[198] IRC §672(f)(2)(A)(i).

2.   The Grantor or the Grantor's spouse is the sole beneficiary of the trust during the life of the Grantor.

3.   The trust was created before September 19, 1995 (regarding assets in trust as of such date) if the trust qualified as a grantor trust, pursuant to Code §676 or Code §677.

Internal Revenue Code §672(f) thus denies NRNC settlors grantor trust status for trusts formed after 1995 unless (i) the grantor retains the right (exercisable either unilaterally or with the consent of another related or subordinate person), to revoke the trust; or (ii) the only amounts permitted to be distributed from the trust during the grantor's life are amounts distributable to the grantor or his spouse.

> One strategy to avoid attribution of trust income to U.S. children is for the NRNC grantor (and the grantor's spouse) to fund a foreign trust pursuant to which distributions are limited to husband and wife.

Foreign assets distributed to the grantor may then be given (tax-free) to a U.S. relative. See page 45. Note that the U.S. done must still report receipt of gifts above $16,388 in 2019 (even if such gifts are not taxable.).[199]

Upon the death of the NRNC grantor, the offshore trust loses its grantor trust status. Trust income from U.S. sources is then recognized by the trust (an independent taxpayer).

Foreign Tax Credit

A foreign non-grantor trust engaged in a U.S. trade or business which pays foreign income tax on income effectively connected to the U.S. business may generally offset such foreign tax against its U.S. income tax liability.[200] Alternatively, the trust may potentially deduct (from U.S. taxable income) such taxes.[201]

---

[199] IRC §672(f)(2)(A)(ii).
[200] See IRC §§901(b((4), 906(a).
[201] See IRC §164(a)(3).

Tax Rates

All U.S. source income earned by a foreign trust is subject to the tax rates applicable to trusts under Code §1(e). The rates are as follows:

Taxable Income	Tax Due
$0 - $2,600	10% of taxable income
$2601 - $9,300	$260 + 24% of the amount over $2,600
$9,301 - $12,750	$1,868 + 35% of the amount over $9,300
$12,751 +	$3,705.50 + 37% of the amount over $12,750

Tax Treaties

Applicable tax treaties may reduce U.S. income tax on foreign (non-grantor) trusts, if the trust is resident in a treaty partner country. For example, most U.S. income tax treaties reduce the tax imposed on passive dividends from 30% to 15%.[202]

---

[202] See page 5.

ESTATE AND GIFT TAX

Funding by U.S. Persons

The lifetime gratuitous transfer of property by a U.S. citizen or resident is generally subject to Gift Tax, apart form the annual $15,000 exclusion per donee. Incomplete gifts (including gifts to trusts) are disregarded for Estate and Gift Tax purposes. NRNCs are subject to Gift Tax on gifts of U.S. situs tangible property. Incomplete gifts remain in the estate of the grantor. (See Completed Gifts, page 20).[203]

Foreign trusts created by U.S. persons are typically "self-settled" (i.e., benefitting the grantor), to utilize the asset protection laws of a foreign jurisdiction. The U.S. settlor typically retains rights to trust income during his lifetime (subject to the foreign trustee's discretion). The Settlor also typically reserves certain powers over trust corpus (i.e., the ability to add or remove new beneficiaries and the right to receive income or principal from the

---

[203] IRC §§2501(q), 2601(a).

trust, subject to trustee discretion). The Code treats such retained rights as preventing completion of the gift (for Gift Tax Purposes).

Such retained rights permit the Settlor to obtain the benefits of foreign protection yet avoid Gift Tax (on the "incomplete" gift).

> To the extent lifetime gifts to an irrevocable trust remain incomplete, Gift Tax is not triggered (but trust assets remain in the grantor's taxable estate). See page 20 above regarding completed gifts.

Incomplete gifts to foreign trusts have no immediate U.S. Estate or Gift Tax consequences. Planning may, however, be required to avoid Estate Tax and the "mark-to-market" deemed sale of trust assts upon the grantor's death (as death causes loss of grantor status). See page 20 above.

Funding by NRNCs

U.S. Gift Tax is imposed on NRNCs only upon the transfer of U.S. situs property to a foreign trust (assuming the transfer is a completed gift).[204] The general strategy of purchasing U.S. assets in a foreign corporation allows for the avoidance of direct gifts and bequests. Limiting trust contributions to equity in a foreign corporation (itself owning U.S. situs assets) is not subject to Gift Tax. See page 42 above. Transfers of foreign situs property by an NRNC to a foreign trust have no legal nexus to (and are not taxed by) the U.S.

---

[204] See IRC §§2001, 2501, 2601.

PRE-IMMIGRATION TAX PLANNING

All NRNCs intending to immigrate to the U.S. should consider planning to avoid recognizing U.S. income, Gift and Estate Tax on worldwide assets. Planning (before establishing U.S. residency) generally involves completing gifts before U.S. residency. See page 20 above.

Pre-Immigration Trusts

Given the worldwide reach of U.S. income, Estate and Gift Taxes on U.S. residents, the most effective tax planning for NRNCs establishes clear and irrevocable asset transfers before the NRNC becomes a U.S. resident.

The funding of an irrevocable foreign trust with foreign assets prior to moving to the United States is an effective tool to avoid Estate and Gift Tax.

> If structured properly, non-U.S. assets transferred to the foreign trust will never be subject to Gift or Estate Tax.

If, however, the NRNC grantor establishes U.S. residency within five years of funding the trust, trust assets may be exposed to U.S. income tax under the Code §684 deemed sale and the Code §679 deemed grantor rules.

Five-Year "Taint" of NRNC Funded Foreign Trust

NRNCs intending to immigrate to the U.S. should take great care to avoid U.S. residency within five years of transferring property to a foreign trust. Internal Revenue Code §679 applies to trusts funded by an NRNC grantor who becomes a U.S. resident within five years of funding.[205] A foreign trust so subject to §679 with U.S. beneficiaries is disregarded, deeming trust assets as owned by the U.S. grantor (for income tax purposes).

The immigrant grantor (who becomes a U.S. resident within five years of funding a foreign trust) is treated as having re-transferred property to the foreign trust on the date of establishing residency, triggering either (i) the deemed sale rules of Code §684 (if the trust has no U.S. beneficiaries) or (ii) grantor status under

---

[205] *See* IRC §679(a)(4); Treas. Reg. §1.679-5(a).

Code §679 (if the foreign trust has a U.S. beneficiary). In the event of deemed grantor status under Code §679, either deemed sale of trust assets (under Code §684) or exposure to the Estate Tax will be triggered upon the death of the immigrating grantor. This outcome may frustrate any advantage of pre-immigration gifting of estate assets to a foreign trust prior to residency.

Reporting

Immigrants deemed by Code §679 to own (for income tax purposes) property transferred to a foreign trust within five years of residency must report such transfers (deemed or actual) on IRS Form 3520. The U.S. residency starting date triggers filing requirements necessary to inform the IRS of facts potentially causing the alter deemed sale of assets held by a foreign trust. Trust income accruing before U.S. residency is not subject to U.S. tax and not reportable (except to the extent of U.S. source income).

Five-Year Period to Determine U.S. Beneficiaries

The determination of whether a foreign trust has U.S. beneficiaries (making the trust disregarded as "grantor" under Code §679) is made annually. A foreign trust created by a U.S. resident as non-grantor (with no U.S. beneficiaries) may become grantor if a beneficiary obtains U.S. residency within 5 years of the grantor funding the trust.[206] The U.S. grantor must recognize all accumulated trust income in the taxable year the NRNC beneficiary becomes a U.S. resident.[207] The U.S. grantor recognizes all income of the foreign trust for each subsequent year the foreign trust remains grantor.

Note that, if a foreign trust ceases to have a U.S. beneficiary, the U.S. grantor is treated as having made a transfer to the foreign trust on the first day of the first taxable year following the last taxable year the trust was treated as having a U.S. beneficiary. The deemed transfer by a U.S. grantor to a foreign trust with no U.S. beneficiary triggers the deemed sale by

---

[206] *See* Treas. Reg. §1.679-2(a)(3).
[207] *See* Treas. Reg. §1.679-2(c)(1).

the grantor or trust assets under Code §684. Trust assets are deemed sold at fair market value (including appreciation since contribution to the trust).[208]

No U.S. Beneficiaries

> Deemed grantor status under Code §679 does not apply to foreign trusts without U.S. beneficiaries.

Potential U.S. beneficiaries and future beneficiaries are, however, counted. For example, if a foreign trust may be amended to add a U.S. person as a beneficiary, trust assets will be deemed recontributed yb an immigrating grantor upon U.S. residency (even if the trust has no actual U.S. beneficiaries). The trust is then deemed a foreign grantor trust, with all income taxable to the immigrant grantor.[209] However, if a foreign beneficiary first becomes a U.S. resident more than five years after the trust is funded, the trust is not treated as having a U.S. beneficiary for

---

[208] *See* Treas. Reg. §1.679-2(c)(2).
[209] Treas. Reg. §1.679-2(a)(4)(ii)A).

purposes of Code §679. The exception is not available if the beneficiary was previously a U.S. resident.[210]

Indirect Transfers

Internal Revenue Code §679 applies to direct as well as indirect transfers.[211] For example, consider a proposed immigrant "A" who gives assets to his brother "B" before moving to the U.S. If B funds a trust for A and his family less than 5 years before A moves to the U.S., A will be treated as the owner of the trust assets for income tax purposes. A's only defense would require proof that B was not acting as an intermediary.[212]

---

[210] *See* Treas. Reg. §1.679-2(a)(3), Ex. 2.
[211] Treas. Reg. §1.679-3(c).
[212] Treas. Reg. §1.679-3(c).

No Transfer Taxes Upon Funding

As noted on page 55 above, with the exception of transfers of U.S. situs tangible property to a foreign trust, U.S. estate and Gift Tax (unlike the applicable U.S. income tax provisions) does not apply to NRNC contributions to a foreign trust. The Estate and Gift Taxes are not triggered by the transfer of foreign property to a foreign trust, even in anticipation of U.S. immigration.[213] The trust is generally treated like an individual NRNC.

Five-Year Lookback Does Not Apply to Transfer Taxes

When an NRNC becomes a U.S. resident within five years of transferring property to a foreign trust, the NRNC grantor is treated (for income tax purposes) as owning the property so transferred (if such trust has a U.S. beneficiary). This provision, however, does not alter the avoidance of Estate or Gift Tax (governed under Subtitle B of the Code). When summarizing Code §679, the U.S. House of Representatives confirmed that:

---

[213] Text refers to Code §§2001, 2501, 2601. (this assumes a completed gift).

"an inter vivos trust which is treated as owned by a U.S. person under this provision [Section 679)] is not treated as owned by the estate of that person upon his death. These rules [only] apply for income tax purposes. Whether the corpus of the inter vivos trust is included in the estate for the U.S. person depends on the estate tax provisions of the Code. Such provisions, as well as the gift tax provisions of the Code, are unaffected by this amendment."[214]

Furthermore, in 2000, the U.S. Treasury issued proposed regulations under Code §679, including Proposed Regulation 1.679-5 for Code §679(a)(4). The proposed regulation is titled "Pre-Immigration Trusts." The preamble to the proposed regulation affirms the original legislative history of the statute, and provides that:

---

[214] *See* P.L. 94-455, Tax Reform Act of 1976, HR. Rpt. No. 658, 94th Cong., 1st Sess. At 209 (Nov. 12, 1975). The Senate Report contains the same language. P.L. 94-455, Tax Reform Act of 1976, S. Rpt. No. 938, 94th Cong., 2nd Sess. At 218 (June 10, 1976). Furthermore, this interpretation was affirmed when the IRS quoted the same language in PLR 9332006 (1992).

"Section 679 applies only for income tax purposes. The estate and gift tax provisions of the Code determine whether a transfer to a foreign trust is subject to the federal gift tax, or whether the corpus of a foreign trust is included in the gross estate of the U.S. transferor."[215]

The 5-year "deemed owner" rule (of Code §679(a)(4)) does not therefore apply for U.S. Estate and Gift Tax purposes. Completed gifts by the NRNC grantor to a foreign trust (removing foreign assets from exposure to U.S. Estate Tax) are therefore respected for Estate and Gift Tax purposes (without regard to the grantor's later U.S. residency).

---

[215] *See* Preamble to Prop. Reg. §1.679-5, 65 F.R. 48185-02 (Aug. 7, 2000).

PRE-IMMIGRATION PLANNING

Tax Planning

Gifting Assets Prior to Residency

U.S. citizens and residents are subject to Estate and Gift Tax on their worldwide assets (without regard to the location of the property). Individuals planning to move to the U.S. should consider avoiding U.S. Estate and Gift Tax by giving assets to non-U.S. family and foreign trusts prior to relocating. Lifetime gifts of foreign property and intangible U.S. property to non-U.S. persons remove the property from Estate Tax forever. Only gifts of U.S. tangible property subject NRNCs to Gift Tax. Pre-immigration gifts remove property from the NRNC's taxable estate and (if properly effected) avoid Gift Tax.

Gifts by NRNCs (before relocation) may be made through irrevocable foreign trusts. Once assets are properly transferred, all trust assets will avoid any later Gift or Estate Tax. If the trust is structured to exclude U.S. beneficiaries and avoid characterization as a "grantor trust," U.S. income tax may also potentially be avoided on future trust income.[216]

Although potentially not as efficient from an income tax perspective, the NRNC anticipating a permanent move to the U.S. should also consider gifts to U.S. residents and citizens. Once given, appreciating assets (if properly transferred, either outright or in trust) avoid any later Gift or Estate Tax.

Note that gifting property to a foreign trust in which the grantor retains an interest may not function to avoid Estate Tax. A retained interest (generally allowing the grantor access to property contributed) may bring trust assets into the immigrant's taxable estate. See page 21 regarding "incomplete" gifts.

Selling Appreciated Assets

Although this book covers only certain aspects of the Estate Tax and Gift Tax, one trap for the unwary immigrant is the U.S. capital gains tax. The tax is incurred by U.S. residents and citizens when gain is realized on the sale of appreciated assets

---

[216] *See* Code §672(f)5((B).

(wherever located). NRNCs are not generally subject to capital gains tax on the sale of U.S. securities. Gains should be incurred (U.S. tax-free) before entering the U.S. Before establishing U.S. residency (or spending at least 130 days in the U.S. during any year), all appreciated liquid securities and (if feasible) other appreciated assets should be sold or gifted.

> Upon becoming a U.S. income tax resident, the immigrant is taxed on all gains realized on the sale of all property wherever located.

To the extent feasible (and defendable), potential immigrants should consider selling appreciated property to related parties. The foreign sales increase the basis held in the property to current fair market value (avoiding future U.S. capital gains tax).

EXPATRIATION

General

Long-term residents who abandon U.S. residency may find themselves entangled in the web of tax provisions applicable to U.S. citizens who expatriate. Non-citizen residents who leave the U.S. may be liable for an "exit tax" on the deemed sale of all assets worldwide.

U.S. citizens may expatriate by renouncing their U.S. nationality at a U.S. embassy or consulate.[217] Non-citizen long-term permanent residents may similarly terminate residency.

> Certain long-term resident non-citizens who exit after at least eight of the last fifteen taxable years in the U.S. are subject to the same tax impact imposed on expatriating citizens (Code §§877(e)(2) or 877A).

---

[217] 8 USC §1481.

135

The "Exit Tax" is an income tax on (i) gain from the deemed sale of worldwide assets on the day prior to expatriation and (ii) the deemed taxable distribution of IRAs, 529 plans, and health savings accounts. Because the Exit Tax deems the taxpayer as either having sold his property or received a distribution of retirement and other accounts (without actually having sold any property), it may create a liquidity shortage (as no actual sales proceeds are available to pay the tax). Under certain circumstances, payment of the tax may be deferred until actual sale of the property (or death).

The current expatriation tax regime consists of two main components – an "Exit Tax" and an "Inheritance Tax." Both taxes are triggered upon termination of citizenship or (for non-citizens) abandonment of long-term residency.

A long-term lawful permanent resident is defined as any individual lawful resident green-card holder during eight of the fifteen years prior to abandonment of the green card.[218] If a green

---

[218] *See* IRC §7701(b)(6), §877-A(g)5) and §877(e)(2).

card holder "expatriates" before this "8 of 15" year test is met, the tax on expatriation does not apply. Thus, a non-green card resident alien (living in the U.S. and taxed on worldwide income) is not subject to the expatriation tax.

Two actions are required to abandon long-term U.S. residency. Long-term residency by a non-citizen is abandoned for immigration purposes only upon formal relinquishment of the resident's green card (after having enjoyed permanent U.S. residency for eight of the fifteen tax years ending with the year of renunciation). A green card holder may abandon permanent U.S. resident status by signing and submitting Form I-407 to a U.S. consulate or U.S. Citizenship and Immigration Services (USCIS) and relinquishing the green card. The application is in Form I-407 or may be made by certified letter of abandonment submitted with the permanent resident card. Although green cards generally expire after ten years, the holder must formally relinquish permanent resident status to avoid remaining a "long-term" U.S. resident for tax purposes.

Long-term residents abandoning residency after June 3, 2004 must also file a tax information statement with the IRS (for any taxable year in which Code Sections 877(b) or 877A[219] applies) on Form 8854 (*Expatriation Information Statement*).[220] Failure to file Form 8854 for the year in which the green card was abandoned and for any tax year to which the expiration tax rules apply could result in fines as high as $10,000 per year.[221]

Expatriation for immigration purposes does not relieve such individual of his or her obligation to file U.S. tax returns and report worldwide income as a citizen or U.S. resident.[222] Until the expatriated individual files Form 8854 and notifies the Department of State or the Department of Homeland Security of his or her expatriating act, the U.S. will continue to tax the

---

[219] IRC §6039G(a), amended by P.L.108-357, §804 and P.L. 110-245, §301(e)(1).
[220] *See* Notice 2009-85, 2009-45 I.R.B 598 (HEART Act Guidance); Notice 2005-36.
[221] IRC §6039G(c). Such penalties may be abated if the taxpayer shows that the failure to file is due to reasonable cause and not to willful neglect.
[222] *See* IRS Instructions for Form 8854.

expatriate. The applicable Treasury Regulation provides that resident status is deemed "abandoned" only when it is "administratively or judicially determined to have been abandoned".[223]

Thus, it may be possible for an expatriate to remain a citizen or resident for tax purposes, taxable on worldwide income, for years after citizenship/residency has been lost for nationality/immigration law purposes.[224] A former long-term resident who fails to notify the IRS of loss of residency could potentially continue to be taxed as a resident in perpetuity (even after surrendering his or her green card to the Department of

---

[223] See Treas. Reg. §301.7701(b)-1(b)(3) (See also *Topsnik v. Commissioner of Internal Revenue* (146 TC 1 (U.S. Tax Ct. 2016), holding that expatriation date was the date on which former lawful permanent resident completed Form I-407 and surrendered his green card) and *Topsnik v. Commissioner of Internal Revenue* (143 TC 240 (U.S. Tax Ct. 2014) (stating that permanent resident status for Federal income tax purposes turns on Federal income tax law and is only indirectly determined by immigration law; recognizes that the Internal Revenue Code and Regulations circumscribe the means by which a permanent resident may abandon that status for federal income tax purposes).
[224] *Id.*; [former IRC §7701(n), effective for any expatriate between 2004-2008].

Homeland Security).[225] Moreover, at death, worldwide assets of the expatriate may be subject to U.S. Estate Tax.[226]

Interestingly, a green-card holder may make an unintended expatriation. An unintended expatriation may occur if the green-card holder becomes a resident of a country which has an income tax treaty with the U.S. If the individual files his or her U.S. income tax return, and, on that return, takes a treaty-based position (as a foreign resident) for tax relief, expatriation (for U.S. tax purposes) occurs.[227] The green card holder is deemed to abandon U.S. permanent residency under Code §7701(b)(6), triggering an expatriation event.

---

[225] *See* former §7701(n)(2).
[226] *Id.*
[227] *Confronting the New Expatriation Tax: Advice for the U.S. Green Card Holder,* Campbell, John L. and Michael J. Stegman, ACTEC Journal 266 (2009), citing IRC §7701(b)(6). I.R.C. §7701(b)(6) provides that "An individual shall cease to be treated as a lawful permanent resident of the U.S. if such individual commences to be treated as a resident of a foreign country under the provisions of a tax treaty between the United States and the foreign country, does not waive the benefits of such treaty applicable to residents of the foreign country, and notifies the Secretary of the commencement of such treatment."

Depending on the year of renunciation, the expatriate may incur U.S. tax under Code §§877 or 877A. The expatriation date determines which set of expatriation tax rules apply. Individuals who expatriated after June 3, 2004 and before June 17, 2008 are subject to a ten-year transition rules under Code §877. The Heroes Earnings Assistance and Relief Tax Act of 2008 (the "HEART Act") added Section 877A, effective for individuals who expatriate on or after June 17, 2008. The HEART Act imposes the newer expatriation tax under Code §877A. As the prior law has waned in relevance, Code §877A is discussed below.

Generally, a nonresident alien becomes a "resident alien" for U.S. tax purposes on the "Residency Start Date" ("RSD"). Pre-immigration tax planning (whether for Estate, Gift or U.S. income tax purposes) cannot generally be accomplished after the RSD. Regarding the U.S. income tax, the RSD is the earlier of (i) the first day the person is present in the U.S. during the year of "substantial presence" (explained below); or (ii) the first day the individual is physically present in the U.S. as a green card holder.

141

For the Estate and Gift Tax, the RSD is the date the individual becomes "domiciled" in the U.S. (i.e., the day a foreign individual relocates to the U.S. with the intent to remain in the U.S. permanently).

For U.S. income tax purposes, the "substantial presence test" classifies a non-citizen as "resident" or "nonresident" (under §7701(b) of the Code and regulations), based on a weighted average of the number of days present in the U.S. in the current and the two preceding years. Any foreign individual is deemed a "resident" for income tax purposes for any calendar year of presence in the U.S., for at least 31 days (the current calendar year) and an average of 183 or more days during the current and two prior years. In calculating the average of the current calendar year and the two preceding calendar years, days during current year are counted at their full value; days present during the immediately preceding calendar year are counted as 1/3 of a day, and days present during the second preceding calendar year are counted as 1/6 of a day. To avoid "resident" alien status for U.S. income tax purposes, presence in the U.S. must be limited to avoid a weighted annual average presence of 183 days.

The "Exit Tax" under §877A (Income Tax)

Internal Revenue Code §877A(a) imposes a "mark-to-market" tax regime on "covered expatriates."

> Under Section 877A(a)(1), all property of a covered expatriate is treated as being sold on the day before his or her expatriation date for its fair market value.[229]

Section 877(a)(2)(A) provides that any gain arising from the deemed sale is taken into account for the taxable year of the deemed sale (at fair market value).[229]

Thus, the "mark to market" regime imposes an income tax on the unrealized gain (on the covered expatriate's worldwide

---

[228] *Topsnik v. Commissioner of Internal Revenue*, 146 T.C. No. 1 (U.S. Tax Ct., 2016) at *12.
[229] *Id.*

assets). The deemed gain is calculated as of the day before the expatriation date, to the extent exceeding a safe harbor threshold ($725,000 for 2019).[230] The rates of tax differ with the type of asset involved. Long-term capital gain assets and qualified dividends receive preferential rates. However, the unrealized gain in a life insurance contract is generally taxed at ordinary income rates. The "exit" tax is generally payable immediately (i.e., April 15 following the close of the tax year in which expatriation occurs).

"Covered Expatriate" Status for §877A – 3 Tests. Internal Revenue Code §877A applies to only "covered expatriates" who meet at least one of the three requirements, or "tests," set out in Section 877(a)(2)(A) – (C).[231]

---

[230] *See* IRC §877A(a)(1) - (3) (calculating the $600,000 safe harbor with yearly inflation).

[231] Note that statutory exceptions may apply to exclude certain persons from "covered expatriate" status (even if the tests are otherwise satisfied). These statutory exceptions pertain to certain persons who are dual citizens at birth and minors who have relinquished U.S. citizenship prior to reaching age 18 ½ years old and have been income tax residents of the U.S. for no more than 10 years within the 15-year period ending with the taxable year of the expatriation.

The Net Worth Test. A person is a "covered expatriate" if his or her net worth is $2,000,000 or more on the date of expatriation. The threshold considers all assets worldwide. For purposes of determining an individual's net worth, all assets subject to Gift Tax (Chapter 12 of the Code), deemed given immediately prior to expatriation, are included.

The Average Annual Income Tax Liability Test. A person is a "covered expatriate" if his or her average annual net income tax for the five years ending before the date of expatriation is more than $171,000 (for 2020) adjusted for inflation. An individual who files a joint tax return must take into account the net income tax reflected on the joint return.[232]

Failure to Certify Tax Compliance. A person is a covered expatriate if "such individual fails to certify (under penalty of perjury) that he or she has met the requirements of this title for the five preceding taxable years or fails to submit evidence of such compliance as the Secretary may require."[233] Although courts

---

[232] Section 2(B) of Notice 2009-85, referencing §III of Notice 97-19.
[233] *Topsnik* at *13, quoting IRC §877A(a)(2)(C).

145

(including the U.S. Tax Court) are not legally bound by the current IRS Notice 2009-85, it is an official statement of the IRS' position, requiring certification of U.S. tax compliance during the five years prior to expatriation (on Form 8854). The Notice may be considered as persuasive authority a court may consider in ruling on compliance with Section 877A.[234]

Even if an individual does not meet either of the two financial tests (the "Net Worth Test" and the "Average Annual Income Tax Liability" test) for covered expatriate status, the failure to file Form 8854 may (at least from the IRS perspective) result in covered expatriate status. Persons without considerable assets or income may nonetheless become exposed to Section 877A by failing to certify tax compliance.

The "Mark to Market" Regime (Calculation of Tax). A covered expatriate is deemed to have sold any interest in property other than property described in Section 877A(c) (deferred compensation, specified tax-deferred accounts and any interest in

---

[234] *Topsnik* at *13.

a non-grantor trust (discussed below)), as of the day before the expatriation date.[235] The property subject to the mark-to-market regime of §877A(a) is of a type whose value would be includible in the value of a decedent's U.S. gross taxable estate (as if the covered expatriate had died on the day before his expatriation date).[236] A covered expatriate is therefore considered to own (for the Exit Tax purposes) and sell the property includable in his or her taxable U.S. estate.

Section 877A(a) requires "proper adjustments" for any gain or loss realized with respect to an asset that is deemed sold under the Exit Tax. Basis is adjusted upward ("stepped up") by the amount of gain attributable to the deemed sale (to avoid double taxation upon the later actual sale of the property). Similarly, basis is reduced to the extent of a deemed loss.[237] Certain types of property held by a long-term resident are ineligible for the step up.

---

[235] Deferred compensation, specified tax-deferred accounts and interest in non-grantor trusts are taxed independently of the mark-to-market tax, under §877A(c).
[236] *Topsnik* at *15.
[237] IRC §877A(a), (h)(2).

For instance, property which would have been taxed if the individual had never become a permanent resident (*e.g.*, U.S. real property interests or property used in connection with a U.S. trade or business) is not eligible for the step-up.[238]

Under §877A(a)(3), if an expatriate's deemed gain is less than an (adjusted for inflation) the annual threshold amount, there is no tax due. For 2020 expatriates, the exemption amount is $737,000. Gain exceeding the exemption must be allocated pro rata among all appreciated property.[239] Such allocation typically involves a complicated process of allocating the exclusion amount among each gain asset (based on the gain applicable to each asset) over the total built-in gain of all gain assets.[240]

---

[238] Notice 2009-85 at Section 3.D.

[239] *See* "Robert W. Wood, *Expatriating and Its U.S. Tax Impact*, by Robert W. Wood, BNA DAILY TAX REPORT, Vo. 2011, No. 17, dated January (Jan. 26, 2011).

[240] *Id.*

The "Inheritance Tax" (IRC Section under §2801)

In addition to the Exit Tax, (triggering the deemed sale of assets upon expatriation), the Heart Act added the Section 2801 "Inheritance Tax" to the Internal Revenue Code.

> The Inheritance Tax imposes a transfer tax (in addition to the Estate Tax, Gift Tax and U.S. Generation Skipping Tax) on lifetime or testamentary gifts by expatriate U.S. citizens and long-term residents.

The "Inheritance Tax" is generally assessed on all property held by "covered expatriates," in additional to the U.S. "Exit Tax." Appreciated property already taxed by the mark-to-market expatriation tax of §877A is thus also subject to the §2801 Inheritance Tax (imposed at the highest Estate and Gift Tax rate).

The Inheritance Tax is imposed on U.S. citizens or residents who receive (from expatriates) property that would otherwise have escaped U.S. Estate or Gift Tax (as a consequence of the donor's expatriation). U.S. recipients are taxed on gifts or

149

bequests by "covered expatriates." Donees subject to Inheritance

Tax include U.S. citizens or residents, domestic trusts, charitable

remainder trusts, foreign trusts electing to be treated as domestic

trusts for the purposes of §2801 and migrated foreign trusts.[241]

The intent of Section 2801 is to ensure that expatriates cannot

avoid U.S. transfer tax on property transferred (after-expatriation)

to U.S. citizens or residents.

Section 2801 imposes what practically amounts to a

second expatriation tax for gifts and bequests by expatriates.

Unlike NRNCs who may gift foreign property to U.S. residents

tax-free, "covered expatriates" are taxed on gifts of assets held

worldwide (even if acquired after expatriation). The §2801

Inheritance Tax is triggered when a "covered expatriate" makes a

"covered gift" or "covered bequest". The Inheritance Tax (unlike

the Estate Tax and Gift Tax) is imposed on the U.S. recipient. The

Tax therefore saddles the donee with what amounts to U.S. Estate

or Gift Tax (otherwise avoided by the expatriate).

---

[241] IRC §2801(b), Prop. Treas. Reg. §28.2801-4(a).

Section 2801 does not expire. Thus, a gift or bequest made by a covered expatriate decades after expatriating may trigger the Inheritance Tax. Currently, the Inheritance Tax rate is 40% of the gross value of the "covered gift" or "covered bequest".[242] All U.S. and non-U.S. situs assets (of the expatriate) are taxed at forty percent (if transferred to a U.S. citizen or resident).

The U.S. recipient (liable for the tax) does not receive an increased tax basis for Inheritance Tax paid. Note, however, that property subject to the mark-to-market regime of §877A does receive a fair market value tax basis. The increased basis transfers to the donee.[243]

A few definitions integral to understanding §2801 are as follows:

"Citizen or resident of the United States." A citizen or resident of the U.S. (subject to the Inheritance Tax) is an

---

[242] §2801(a); Prop. Treas. Reg. §28.2801-4(b).
[243] §877A(a); *See also* Paragraph C of Section 3, IRS Notice 2009-85 (November 9, 2009).

individual who is a citizen or non-citizen Estate and Gift Tax resident of the U.S. at the time of the covered gift or covered bequest.[244] U.S. citizens also includes domestic trusts (as defined under §7701(a)(30)(E)), as well as foreign trusts electing to be treated as a domestic trust.[245]

"Covered gift or bequest." A gift by an expatriate generally becomes a "covered gift or bequest" if (i) acquired by gift, directly or indirectly, from an individual who, at the time of such acquisition, is a "covered expatriate" (even if mark-to-market tax is paid under §877A) when received by a U.S. citizen or resident or (ii) property acquired directly or indirectly by reason of the death of an individual who, immediately before death (even if mark-to-market tax is paid under §877A), was a "covered expatriate." The determination of whether a gift is a covered gift is made without regard to the situs of the property and whether

---

[244] Accordingly, whether an individual is a "resident" is based on domicile (presence in the United States and an intent to remain), notwithstanding that §877A adopts the income tax definition of the term.

[245] Prop. Treas. Reg. §28.2801-2(b); Prop. Treas. Reg. §28.2801-5(d).

such property was acquired by the covered expatriate before or after expatriation.[246] Note that gift of intangible assets (otherwise exempt from Estate and Gift Tax, if made by NRNCs) and gifts of less value than the annual $15,000 Gift Tax exclusion are not excluded from the definition of a "covered gift" under §2801.[247]

"U.S. Recipient." Includes U.S. citizens, U.S. domiciliaries, domestic trusts, electing foreign trusts and U.S. interest-holders of a domestic entity that receives a covered gift or covered bequest.[248] For purposes of §2801, an individual donee of a covered gift or bequest is a "resident", if domiciled in the U.S.[249] If a person falls within the definition, they are a "covered beneficiary" under §2801.

Under proposed regulations, the following transfers are exempt from the application of the §2801 Inheritance Tax:

---

[246] Prop. Treas. Reg. §28.2801-2(f).
[247] Prop. Treas. Reg. §28.2801-3(c)(1).
[248] Prop. Treas. Reg. §28.2801-2(e).
[249] Prop. Treas. Reg. §28.2801-2(b).

Reportable Taxable Gifts. A taxable gift reported on the donor's timely filed Form 709 Gift Tax Return is not a "covered gift" under §2801.

Property Subject to the Estate Tax. Property included in the gross estate of the "covered expatriate" and timely reported and paid is not subject to Inheritance Tax.

Transfers to Charities. Charitable gifts (described in §2522(b) of the Code) and bequests (described in §2055(a)) are not "covered gifts" or "covered bequests", to the extent a charitable deduction under §2522 or §2055 of the Code would have been allowed if the "covered expatriate" had been a U.S. citizen or resident at the time of transfer.[250] Charitable giving may therefore be a viable strategy to avoid the Inheritance Tax.

Transfers to Spouse. A transfer from a "covered expatriate" to the covered expatriate's spouse is not a "covered gift" or "covered bequest", to the extent a marital deduction under

---

[250] Prop. Treas. Reg. §28.2801-3(c)(3); IRC §2801(e)(3).

§2523 or §2056 would have been allowed if the "covered expatriate" had been a U.S. citizen or resident at the time of the transfer.[251]

Qualified Disclaimers. A transfer pursuant to a qualified disclaimer of property by a "covered expatriate" (defined in §2518(b) of the Code), is not a "covered gift" or "covered bequest."[252] A qualified disclaimer is a written refusal of a gift or bequest by the designated beneficiary (i.e., the gifting expatriate) within nine months of the intended transfer to the beneficiary. To be effective, the designated beneficiary must not accept the interest or any of its benefits, and the interest must pass without any direction on the part of the person making the qualified disclaimer.[253]

The §2801 Inheritance Tax is calculated by multiplying the "net covered gifts and covered bequests" received by a U.S. recipient during the calendar year by the highest Estate Tax or Gift

---

[251] Prop. Treas. Reg. §28.2801-3(c)(4).
[252] Prop. Treas. Reg. §28.2801-3(c)(5).
[253] IRC §2518(b).

Tax rate for the applicable calendar year.[254] "Net covered gifts and covered bequests" include all such gifts and bequests received by the U.S. recipient during the calendar year, less the §2801(c) annual exclusion amount per-donee (currently $15,000).[255]

For example, in Year 1, A, a U.S. citizen, receives a $50,000 covered gift from B and an $80,000 covered bequest from C. Both B and C are covered expatriates. In Year 1, the highest estate and gift tax rate is forty percent and the Code Section 2801(c) annual exempt amount is $15,000. A's Inheritance Tax for Year 1 is computed by multiplying A's net covered gifts and covered bequests by forty percent. A's net covered gifts and covered bequests for Year 1 are $115,000, which is determined by reducing A's total covered gifts and covered bequests received during Year 1, $130,000 ($50,000 + $80,000), less $15,000 [the §2801(c) exemption amount for 2018]. A's §2801 tax liability is then reduced by any foreign estate or gift tax paid under §2801(e). Assuming A, B, and C paid no foreign estate or gift tax on the

---

[254] Prop. Treas. Reg. §28.2801-4(b)(1).
[255] Prop. Treas. Reg. §28.2801-4(b)(2).

transfers, A's §2801 tax liability for Year 1 is $46,000 ($115,000 x 40%).

Determining Tax Basis for Payment of §2801 Inheritance Tax. The U.S. recipient's basis in a "covered gift" or "covered bequest," remains governed by Code Sections 1015 and 1014.[256] As property forming a "covered bequest" is technically not included in the expat's taxable gross estate, the property acquired by the U.S. recipient will not receive a tax basis step-up to fair market value (regardless of the §2801 Inheritance Tax paid).[257] "Covered gifts" are governed by the gift tax basis rules and maintain a carryover basis from the expat donor.[258] While Code §1015(d) generally permits a basis step-up on the amount of gift tax paid, it does not apply for any tax paid under §2801 for "covered gifts."[259]

---

[256] Prop. Treas. Reg. §28.2801-6(a).

[257] Treas. Reg. §1.1014-2(b)(2) – the fair market value basis step-up under §1014(a) does not apply for "property not includible in the decedent's gross estate such as property not situated in the United States acquired from a nonresident who is not a citizen of the United States."

[258] Treas. Reg. §1.1015-1(a).

[259] Treas. Reg. §1.1015-5.

§2801 Tax Treatment of Foreign Trusts. A foreign trust (absent an election to be treated as a domestic trust) which receives a "covered gift" or "covered bequest" is not liable for the Inheritance Tax. U.S. beneficiaries of the trust are, however, liable for the Inheritance Tax upon receipt of distributions from the foreign trust, to the extent attributable[260] to a "covered gift" or "covered bequest." Trust beneficiaries therefore incur the tax upon receipt of covered gifts initially contributed to the foreign trust.[261]

Distributions to U.S. beneficiaries may be partially attributable to covered gifts. In such case the covered portion (subject to §2801 tax) is determined by multiplying the fair market value of the distribution, as of December 31 of the preceding tax year, by a §2801 tax ratio which generally apportions the distribution based on the ratio of "covered gift" to non-covered

---

[260] As determined by Prop. Treas. Reg. §28.2801-5(b) and (c).
[261] Prop. Treas. Reg. §28.2801-4(a)(3); Prop. Treas. Reg. §28.2801 – 4(a)3).

gift property in the trust.[262] If valid records are not available, the §2801 Inheritance Tax is imposed on the entire trust corpus.[263]

Domestic trusts are treated as U.S. citizens under §2801, immediately liable for tax upon receipt of a covered gift.[264] IF a foreign trust elects to be treated as a domestic trust under §2801, the Inheritance Tax is due on all "covered gifts" and "covered bequests" received in the calendar year of the election (i.e. the year Form 708 is filed).[265] If the electing foreign trust received "covered gifts" or "covered bequests" during years prior to electing domestic trust status, it must also report and pay Inheritance Tax on such property's fair market value.[266]

---

[262] *Id.*
[263] *Id.*
[264] IRC §2801(e)(4()A).
[265] Prop. Treas. Reg. §28.2801-5(d).
[266] Prop. Treas. Reg. §28.201-5(d)(3)(iii).

TAX REPORTING

Both resident and non-resident non-citizens are subject to a number of IRS reporting requirements. Several significant filing requirements are outlined below.

Residents

Schedule B of Form 1040. The Internal Revenue Code generally requires U.S. citizens and resident aliens to report all worldwide income, including income from foreign trusts and foreign bank and securities accounts. Part III of Schedule B (Foreign Accounts and Trusts) requires specific disclosure of foreign accounts, including the country in which each account is held.

Form 709, United States Gift (and Generation-Skipping Transfer) Tax Return. A U.S. person who transfers money or property to an individual or trust may be required to file Form 709.

FinCEN Form 114, Report of Foreign Bank and Financial Accounts ("FBAR"). The Bank Secrecy Act requires U.S. persons (any U.S. citizen, green card holder or any individual that satisfies the Code's substantial presence test for residents) to disclose any financial interest in or signature authority over a foreign financial account, including a bank account, brokerage account, mutual fund, trust, or other type of foreign financial account with a value exceeding $10,000. The Act requires the U.S. person to annually report the account to the IRS on FinCEN Form 114. This "FBAR" is not filed with any tax return. The FBAR is filed on or before April 15 following the tax year during which the account was opened and (thereafter) owned.

FACTA Form 8938, Statement of Special Foreign Financial Assets. The Foreign Account Tax Compliance Act requires U.S. citizens, resident aliens and certain nonresident aliens to report specified foreign financial assets on Form 8938, if the aggregate value exceeds certain thresholds. This includes (1) any financial account maintained by a foreign trust/entity; (2) stock or security issued by other than a U.S. person; (3) any interest in foreign entity; or (4) any trust instrument or contract that has an issuer or counterpart that is not a U.S. person. Form

162

8938 must be filed with the individual's U.S. income tax return for the tax year during which the asset was acquired and (thereafter) owned.

Form 3520, Annual Return to Report Transactions with Foreign Trusts and Receipt of Certain Foreign Gifts. U.S. citizens and residents must report all gifts received from (i) NRAs or any foreign estate, if exceeding $100,000 in the aggregate and (ii) foreign companies, if exceeding $16,649 (adjusted annually for inflation) in the aggregate. Gifts from related parties must be aggregated. For example, if a U.S. resident or citizen receives $60,000 from one NRA and $50,000 from a different NRA during the same year, and the two NRAs are related, the U.S. person must report the gifts (as they aggregate to more than $100,000). The disclosure is made in Part IV of Form 3520. Gifts from foreign trusts are treated as trust distributions (report in Part III of Form 3520). Form 3520 is filed separately from the U.S. income tax return. Form 3520 is due the fifteenth day of the 4th month following the end of the

U.S. person's tax year. If a U.S. person is granted an extension of time to file an income tax return, the due date for filing Form 3520 is the fifteenth day of the 10th month following the end of the U.S. person's tax year.[267]

NRAs

Form 1040NR, U.S. Non-Resident Alien Income Tax Return.

A foreign individual or foreign trust (not disregarded for tax purposes), may be obligated to file Form 1040NR, to disclose and pay tax on U.S. source income.[268]

Foreign Trusts

Form 3520, Annual Return to Report Transactions with Foreign Trusts and Receipt of Certain Foreign Gifts.

Any U.S. person who creates a foreign trust or who transfers property to a foreign trust (generally excluding independent service providers), must report the trust creation or property transfer on IRS Form 3520. Form 3520 is due with the reporting U.S.

---

[267] *See* IRC §6039F; IRS Notice 97-43.
[268] *See* Publication 519.

person's income tax return (for the year of trust creation or funding). Failure to file may subject the transferor to a penalty of 35% of the amount transferred to the trust. Form 3520 is required to be filed by any U.S. person who:

- Creates or transfers money or property to a foreign trust.

- Receives (directly or indirectly) any distribution from a foreign trust.

- Receives certain gifts or bequests from foreign entities.

- Is treated as the U.S. owner of a foreign trust. "Owners" include any U.S. person who creates a foreign trust or is treated as the owner of any assets held by the foreign trust under §671-§679.

All gratuitous transfers to a foreign trust are reportable by the owner of the trust under I.R.C. §684 (on Form 3520A).

Cost payments, such as trustee fees, are not reportable. A beneficiary who receives a payment for services or property in excess of the market value of such services or property is, however, deemed to receive a distribution. Thus, if trustee fees paid to a beneficiary/trustee are excessive, the distribution becomes reportable. The reporting obligation is waived if the payee service provider reports the amount received as taxable compensation for services rendered.

Indirect and constructive distributions are also reportable on Form 3520A. For example, if a beneficiary uses a credit card and the trust guarantees or pays the invoice, the amount charged is considered a distribution.

Form 3520-A, Annual Information Return of Foreign Trust with a U.S. Owner. Form 3520-A provides information about the foreign trust, its U.S. Beneficiaries, and any U.S. person treated as an "owner" of the foreign trust. Each U.S. owner is responsible for ensuring that the foreign trust files Form 3520-A and furnishes required annual statements to U.S. owners and beneficiaries. The foreign trust must file Form 3520-A on or before each March 15 following the reporting year. If Form 3520-

A is not filed, the U.S. owner may be liable for a penalty of 5% of the value of trust assets (deemed owned by each such "owner").[269]

Schedule B of Form 1040 (Part III, Foreign Accounts and Trusts). Schedule B must be completed by any U.S. person who receives a distribution from, is grantor of, or a transferor to a foreign trust. Any U.S. person treated as the owner (within the meaning of Code §671) of a foreign trust is required to file an annual income tax return describing all trust activities and operations.[270] As noted, the U.S. "owner" is also required to disclose on Form 3520 the existence of the trust, its taxpayer identification number, the names of other persons considered "owners" of the trust, the Code section which treats the trust as owned by U.S. person(s), the country in which the trust was created and the date of creation. Form 3520 (as noted above) is due with the deemed owner's U.S. tax return.

If a U.S. "owner" of a foreign trust transfers property to the foreign trust at his death, or whose estate includes (for estate

---

[269] *See* IRC §6677.
[270] *See* IRC §6048.

tax purposes) any portion of a foreign trust, the estate of the U.S. person must report the bequest on Form 3520. Form 3520 is due with decedent's last income tax return. Failure to file may subject the executor to a penalty equal to 35% of the amount transferred.

A U.S. trust that becomes a foreign trust is required to report the change of status on Form 3520, with the trust's income tax return covering the year of the transfer. Failure to file may subject the trust to a penalty equal to 35% of trust assets.

Any U.S. person (including a grantor) who receives, directly or indirectly, any distribution from a foreign trust must report the name of the trust, the amount of distributions received from the trust, and such other information as the Service may require.[271] Reporting is made on Form 3520-A Foreign Grantor Trust Beneficiary Statement or a Foreign Non-Grantor Trust Beneficiary Statement.[272]

---

[271] *See* IRC §6048(c).

[272] *See* Notice 97-34, describing the required information in detail.

CONCLUSION

Non-resident non-citizens are subject to U.S. Estate and Gift Tax only on assets located in the U.S. U.S. intangible property may, however, be gifted by NRNCs free from Gift Tax. The limited $60,000 Estate Tax credit afforded NRNCs mandates prudent planning and meticulous ownership structuring of U.S. assets. Planning includes (i) gifting U.S. intangible property, (ii) acquisition of U.S. assets exempt from Gift and Estate Tax, (iii) ownership of U.S. situs assets through foreign entities (equity in which is not subject to Estate or Gift Tax) and (iv) utilization of Estate and Gift Tax treaties.

U.S. residents and citizens are subject to Estate and Gift Tax on assets held worldwide. To avoid worldwide taxation as a resident, NRNCs should minimize time spent in the U.S. and make clear intentions to return home. Once a non-citizen is taxed as a resident, great care should be taken to avoid exposure to the "exit tax" or related "inheritance tax" upon permanently leaving the U.S.

169

Planning is also integral for the NRNC contemplating immigration to the U.S. If immigration is planned, appreciated property may be sold or gifted prior to U.S. residency (to avoid later Gift, Estate and U.S. capital gains tax). Depending on the wealth of the proposed immigrant, other valuable property (particularly property offshore) should be given away or sold prior to becoming subject to worldwide Gift and Estate Tax.

The Estate and Gift Tax credit is currently substantial for U.S. residents and citizens. Lifetime and testamentary gifts to non-citizen spouses must, however, be carefully planned. The marital exemption for lifetime gifts to noncitizen spouses is very limited. No marital deduction is available for testamentary transfers to noncitizen spouses, unless made through a restrictive QDOT trust.

***

International tax planning should be undertaken solely with the consultation of an attorney experienced in the area.